The Roman Empire: A Very Short Introduction

VERY SHORT INTRODUCTIONS are for anyone wanting a stimulating and accessible way into a new subject. They are written by experts, and have been translated into more than 45 different languages.

The series began in 1995, and now covers a wide variety of topics in every discipline. The VSI library now contains over 500 volumes—a Very Short Introduction to everything from Psychology and Philosophy of Science to American History and Relativity—and continues to grow in every subject area.

Titles in the series include the following:

Christopher Kelly

THE ROMAN EMPIRE

A Very Short Introduction

OXFORD

UNIVERSITY PRESS

Great Clarendon Street, Oxford OX2 6DP

Oxford University Press is a department of the University of Oxford.
It furthers the University's objective of excellence in research, scholarship,
and education by publishing worldwide in

Oxford New York

Auckland Cape Town Dar es Salaam Hong Kong Karachi
Kuala Lumpur Madrid Melbourne Mexico City Nairobi
New Delhi Shanghai Taipei Toronto

With offices in

Argentina Austria Brazil Chile Czech Republic France Greece
Guatemala Hungary Italy Japan Poland Portugal Singapore
South Korea Switzerland Thailand Turkey Ukraine Vietnam

Oxford is a registered trade mark of Oxford University Press
in the UK and in certain other countries

Published in the United States
by Oxford University Press Inc., New York

British Library Cataloguing in Publication Data

Data available

Library of Congress Cataloging in Publication Data

Data available

ISBN 978-0-19-280391-7

Impression: 23

Typeset by RefineCatch Ltd, Bungay, Suffolk

Printed and bound by
CPI Group (UK) Ltd, Croydon, CR0 4YY

Contents

Acknowledgements

To George Miller whose idea this first was; to Mary Beard and John Henderson who gave such valuable advice at its inception; to Marsha Filion, Justin Pollard, and Helen Morales who helped it on its way; to Tony and Jan Leaver, Zachary Watts, Richard Flower, and Caroline Vout who greatly improved it; to James Thompson and Luciana O'Flaherty who saw it safely through to the end.

List of illustrations

The publisher and the author apologize for any errors or omissions
in the above list. If contacted they will be pleased to rectify these at
the earliest opportunity.

Introduction

The Roman empire was a remarkable achievement. At its height, in the 2nd century AD, it had a population of around 60 million people spread across 5 million square kilometres (roughly 20 times the area of the United Kingdom). Then the empire stretched from Hadrian's Wall in drizzle-soaked northern England to the sun-baked banks of the Euphrates in Syria; from the great Rhine-Danube river system, which snaked across the fertile, flat lands of Europe from the Low Countries to the Black Sea, to the rich plains of the North African coast and the luxuriant gash of the Nile valley in Egypt. The empire completely encircled the Mediterranean. This was the Romans' internal lake, complacently referred to by its conquerors as *mare nostrum* – 'our sea'.

This book aims (briefly) to explore some significant aspects of this imperial super-state. Its approach is resolutely thematic; not through any dislike of chronology (see pp. 138–140), but because there are already a good number of useful accounts both of the narrative history of the Roman empire and of the reigns of individual emperors. This book takes a different path across the same territory. Chapter 1 looks at the brutal process of conquest, at the establishment of empire, and at the Romans' sense of their own imperial mission. Chapter 2 considers the presentation of imperial power: it looks at emperors both as gods (in the promotion of the imperial cult) and as men (in the often unflattering histories of

Suetonius and Tacitus). Chapter 3 shifts perspective in order to understand the workings of empire from the point of view of the privileged elites in the cities of the Mediterranean. It was these wealthy men – rather than some vast imperial administration – who were principally responsible for the orderly government of the provinces.

Chapter 4 exploits some of the less well-known literature of the 2nd century AD, written by Greeks under Roman rule. These are precious texts. They offer a sense – rarely recoverable for pre-modern empires – of how those who were conquered sought to establish an identity in a new imperial world. In the Roman empire disputes about the present were often conducted through debates about the past. History-writing was not an isolated, academic exercise; rather, it directly engaged with the language of politics and power. The present may have been resolutely Roman, but the past was still to be fought over.

Chapter 5 turns to consider the growth of the most important group of outsiders in the Roman empire. Christians and their faith were fundamentally shaped by their experiences on the margins of society. By contrast, Chapter 6 offers an insider view, seeking to establish some sense of what it might have been like to live and die in the towns and fields of this huge pre-industrial empire. Chapter 7, the final chapter, looks back at Rome from three modern perspectives: from the British empire in the decade before the First World War, from the fascist Italy of Mussolini, and from Hollywood. These views are important. In a number of significant (and sometimes surprising) ways, they still determine how, at the beginning of the 21st century, the Roman empire is both imagined and judged. Certainly, it is one of the privileges of the present to be able to look back selectively at the past. But equally – as with this Very Short Introduction – it is always important to be aware of that selectivity.

This book concentrates on the Roman empire at the peak of its prosperity. For the most part, it focuses on two centuries, roughly 31 BC to AD 192: from the victory of the future emperor Augustus over Antony and Cleopatra at the Battle of Actium to the assassination of the emperor Commodus. (Although Chapter 1 looks back to the Punic Wars, and Chapter 5 briefly looks forward to the beginning of the 4th century AD, in order to conclude with the conversion of Constantine, the first Roman emperor publicly to support Christianity.)

The principal concern of the following chapters is to understand Rome's achievement in establishing and maintaining one of the largest world empires, and the only one to have embraced northern Europe, the Middle East, and North Africa. That success in itself demands a rich and complex explanation. Only then is it possible to begin to understand the reasons for the subsequent weakening of Roman power, the eventual break-up of the empire in the West into barbarian kingdoms, and the gradual emergence of Byzantium in the East. These themes run far beyond the compass of this book. The best account of that 'awful revolution' remains the magisterial treatment of Edward Gibbon, *The History of the Decline and Fall of the Roman Empire* (London, 1776–1788). But the unwary enthusiast should take note: at six substantial volumes, it was never Gibbon's intention to offer anything approaching a very short introduction.

Chapter 1
Conquest

Expansion and survival

Rome was a warrior state. Its vast empire had been hard won in a series of fiercely fought campaigns. In the 4th century BC Rome – then an unremarkable city – secured its survival through a complex network of alliances with surrounding peoples. A series of victories allowed the Romans to establish their own territory along the Tiber valley and to expand their sphere of influence southwards into Campania (around the Bay of Naples). This was a slow process of gradual advance and steady consolidation. Notable breakthroughs came with the defeat of the Samnites in 295 BC (leading to the extension of Roman control into central Italy) and the thwarted invasion of Pyrrhus, the ruler of Epirus, a kingdom on the Adriatic coast of Greece. In 280 BC Pyrrhus landed his army at Tarentum (modern Taranto on the 'heel' of Italy); despite initial success, he was unable to force a Roman surrender. After five years' campaigning in Sicily and southern Italy, rather than stretch his limited resources and risk defeat, Pyrrhus withdrew.

By the middle of the 3rd century BC, most of the Italian peninsula was under Roman control. In the next hundred years the Romans and their allies challenged the North African city of Carthage, the dominant power in the western Mediterranean. A fleet of merchant ships guaranteed Carthage's continued prosperity and international influence: sailing east to Egypt and Lebanon to trade in luxury goods; north, perhaps as far as Britain, to purchase tin; and south along the African coast to bring back ivory and gold. Against this threatening rival, three long conflicts – known as the Punic Wars – stretched the Romans to their limits. The immediate cause of the First Punic War (264–241 BC) was a dispute over Sicily. The Romans regarded the escalating Carthaginian military presence on the island as a direct threat to their own security. Yet no serious opposition could be offered without an effective means to counter Carthage's command of the seas. The Romans, whose victories in Italy had been based on the superiority of their army, were forced to build a permanent navy. Soldiers were hurriedly retrained as sailors. Later tradition would claim that skilled carpenters had copied the construction of an enemy vessel which had run aground, building 100 ships in 60 days. In the end, this risky strategy paid off. In 241 BC, after 23 years of bitter warfare, the Romans were finally able to enforce a complete Carthaginian withdrawal.

An uneasy peace lasted little more than 20 years. In the Second Punic War (218–201 BC), the great Carthaginian general Hannibal, in one of the most daring and imaginative military campaigns in the ancient world, marched his army of 50,000 men, 9,000 cavalry, and 37 elephants from Spain, across southern France, and over the Alps into Italy. Fewer than half the men survived the journey. Seven months later, in May 217, in the early morning mist, Hannibal trapped the Roman general Flaminius and his troops at Lake Trasimene in Umbria, killing 15,000 men. The following year he nearly wiped out the Roman army at Cannae in Apulia. This was the severest defeat ever inflicted on the Romans. In one battle they lost 50,000 men: the highest death-toll for an army in a single day's fighting in the history of European warfare. And unlike the casualties at the Somme, the Roman soldiers at Cannae fell in hand-to-hand combat, their corpses piled high across a bloody plain.

Hannibal occupied Italy for 15 years. Under the command of Fabius

Maximus – admiringly nicknamed Cunctator, 'the Delayer' – the Romans and their allies deliberately avoided pitched battles. Instead, they burned their own crops and retreated to fortified towns. Slowly starved by this scorched-earth policy, and harried by Roman raiding parties, Hannibal's army was forced to abandon the campaign. The Romans were victorious, but not for a long decade after Cannae. It was not until 202 that Hannibal, recalled to defend Carthage, was defeated at the battle of Zama (in modern Tunisia) by Scipio Africanus. Sixty years later a revived Rome returned to eliminate a much weakened and demoralized Carthage. The Third Punic War (149–146 BC) ended with the complete destruction of the city. Its buildings were systematically levelled and most of its 50,000 surviving inhabitants enslaved.

Expansion westward into Spain and North Africa was matched by war in the East. By 146 BC – the year in which both Carthage and Corinth were sacked – all the major cities in the Balkan peninsula were subject to Rome. In the following century, after a series of difficult campaigns, Asia Minor was finally secured; in the 60s the successful general Pompey 'the Great' annexed Syria; in the 50s Julius Caesar conquered Gaul (from the Pyrenees in southern France to the Rhine); in 31 BC his adopted son Octavian defeated Cleopatra VII, the last independent ruler of Egypt. That victory in a naval battle off Actium in north-western Greece brought the greatest prize. Egypt, the oldest and wealthiest kingdom in the Mediterranean, was now fully part of the Roman empire.

In the wars against Carthage and in the East Rome's traditional, republican system of government had worked tolerably well. Indeed, the 2nd century BC, with its string of military conquests, is conventionally regarded as the apogee of the Roman Republic. Yet, in some ways, 'Republic' is a misleading term. It risks implying – at least for modern readers – too great a degree of popular participation in politics. (This is not an ancient difficulty; the Latin *res publica* is best translated simply as 'affairs of state'.) The Roman Republic was an unabashed plutocracy; the citizen-body was carefully graded according to stringent property qualifications. In turn, this classification regulated voting rights: all adult male citizens were enfranchised, but a system of electoral colleges guaranteed that the rich, if united, would always be able to out-vote the poor. In addition, the heavy costs of electioneering and office-holding ensured that all who were most prominent in government were themselves personally wealthy.

Under this tightly oligarchic constitution two consuls – the most powerful officials in the state – were elected each year. Only those who had held the praetorship (the next most senior magistracy) and were at least 42 years old were permitted to stand. During his term in office a consul might expect an important military command which could then be extended for further annual terms. At the expiry of his stint in the field, an ex-consul relinquished his commission and returned to the Senate, not a directly elected body, but rather an advisory council made up of all those who had held senior magistracies. This pattern of annual office-holding, age-restricted eligibility, and time-limited military commands enforced some degree of collective power-sharing amongst the Roman ruling elite. In the late 3rd and 2nd centuries BC about half the consuls came from ten extended families; an indication not only of the stable dominance of a small hereditary group, but also of a considerable degree of fluidity outside this core. Men without recent senatorial ancestry – or none at all – regularly reached the Senate in large numbers.

The republican constitution also imposed a deliberate restraint on any ambitious individual. Above all, it prevented the long-term concentration of political or military authority in the hands of victorious generals. The true test of a great man – at least for Roman moralists – was not his ability to achieve high office, but his open-handed willingness to relinquish it. When Rome was first struggling to establish itself in Italy, one of its most important battles was won under the leadership of Quinctius Cincinnatus. Cincinnatus (so the story goes) had been loath to leave his fields and interrupt his ploughing in order to raise an army. Even more celebrated than his lack of enthusiasm for high office, was Cincinnatus' refusal to extend his command. Turning his back on the possibility of continued power, he returned to his smallholding and to his plough.

Despite such outstanding exemplars, some of the generals responsible for annexing the richest parts of the Mediterranean proved increasingly reluctant to retire. For these men the tale of Cincinnatus held no moral force. In the end, the restrictions on the exercise of power imposed by the constitution of a republican city-state proved too weak to withstand the extensive ambitions of empire. In the 1st century BC a series of conquering commanders were determined to exploit their success. They held consulships well below the minimum age; they compelled the Senate to renew their military commissions; they relied on the personal loyalty of their troops and the threat of violence to enforce their continued active involvement in politics. When Julius Caesar completed his tour of duty in Gaul he refused to stand down, as he was constitutionally required to do. In January 49, at the head of his army of veterans battle-hardened after eight years of campaigning, he crossed the River Rubicon (which marked the southern territorial limit of his command) and marched on Rome. It was now clear that Caesar's authority rested on military might. Some were prepared to oppose this *coup d'état*, and by equally illegal means. Caesar's assassination five years later, on the Ides of March 44 BC, need not be seen as a virtuous bid for liberty on the part of Brutus and Cassius. (Shakespeare's version should be put firmly to one side.) It was rather a brutal attempt by one oligarchic faction to wrench political control away from a rival.

The result was two decades of civil war. Brutus and Cassius were defeated by an alliance of Mark Antony (one of Caesar's closest associates) and Octavian (Caesar's adopted son). In turn, this fragile partnership collapsed. Antony sought help in Egypt and the support of its ruler, Cleopatra. That was a shrewd move. The wealth of Egypt might be used to fund a war against Octavian; its most important city, Alexandria on the Nile delta, might become a new capital for an eastern Roman empire. These were serious propositions. It is Octavian's slanderous attacks which presented Mark Antony as a drunken, lovesick incompetent caught in the sexual snares of a sensuous Egyptian queen. Such derogatory inventions are the prerogative of the victorious. The destruction of the Egyptian fleet at Actium in 31 BC and Antony's suicide the following year secured Octavian's position and smeared his rival's reputation. Under the newly fabricated title of Augustus – 'the divinely favoured one' – Octavian's command of the riches and military resources of empire allowed him to establish his family as the unchallenged rulers of the Mediterranean world.

The rapid growth of the Roman empire from the mid 2nd century BC was itself the cause of the establishment of a dynastic monarchy just over a century later. But it would be over-hasty to see that shift as the replacement of freedom by autocracy or of independence by tyranny. Under the emperors, from Augustus on, Roman politics was dominated by privileged families who competed, as they had always done, for the spoils of empire. What had changed was how that rivalry might be regulated and how those at court close to an emperor might seek to embrace or exclude those in the provinces whose wealth demanded their incorporation into a new empire-wide aristocracy.

From that point of view, the transfiguration of Octavian into Augustus – the successful conversion of a warlord into an emperor – was less a fracturing of the fundamental nature of Roman politics than the hard-fought reorganization of power amongst a highly competitive oligarchy. The real Roman revolution was the founding of an empire under the Republic. It is perhaps unsurprising too that after Augustus the acquisition of new territories was strictly limited. Campaigns in Britain, Dacia (roughly modern Romania), and Mesopotamia were led by emperors themselves. Other military commands were strictly controlled; potential competitors, even within the imperial household, were carefully policed. This was a severe lesson in risk management well learned. As the vicious civil wars of the 1st century BC had starkly demonstrated, the glittering prizes of Mediterranean conquest might have made even a Cincinnatus hesitate to return to his plough.

Shock and awe

The expansion of a small city-state into an imperial superpower is by any measure an impressive transformation. Rome's empire was secured by an immense military effort which far surpassed any of its opponents, particularly after the defeat of Hannibal. In the 2nd century BC, in order to field an army of around 130,000 men, the Romans not only depended heavily on their Italian allies, but also enlisted around 13% of their own adult male citizens. The call-up fell disproportionately on the young. To sustain an army of such a size required the regular enrolment of 60% of all 17-year-olds for seven years. In other words, over half of all Roman male citizens might expect to serve in the army until their mid-20s. These are extraordinary statistics. A similar commitment of human resources would not be seen again in pre-industrial Europe until the armies of Frederick the Great of Prussia and Napoleon, and then only for a fraction of the two centuries (from the Punic Wars to Actium) of Rome's conquest of the Mediterranean world. To give some rough order of magnitude: to match the Roman investment in military manpower, the modern USA would need to maintain a standing army of just under 13 million serving soldiers, well over ten times its current strength.

This huge military establishment created its own dynamic. In its rigorous discipline, in the superior quality of its weapons, and in the campaign experience of its troops, the Roman army exploited the advantages of scale and repeated success. Victory yielded huge quantities of booty. In turn, the riches plundered from defeated enemies, supplemented with revenue from provincial taxation, funded the heavy cost of continued conquest. The wealth generated by Rome's wars in the eastern Mediterranean was fabled. In 50 years (200–150 BC) the rough equivalent in value of over 30 metric tons of gold was seized. The consolidation of Roman power in Asia Minor and the annexation of Syria meant that even these sums could be exceeded. In 62 BC the victorious Pompey returned from the East with booty worth nearly 70 tons of gold. Fifteen years later, the glut of gold extracted by Julius Caesar from Gaul caused the price to drop sharply.

The acquisition of empire was nowhere more loudly acclaimed than in Rome itself. The centre of the city was crammed with monuments glorifying the advance of Roman rule: grand victory arches, imposing statues, temples brilliantly emblazoned with the spoils of war. Roman historians packed their lengthy narratives with a seemingly endless succession of campaigns and battles. In the 2nd century BC all those seeking public office were required to have served in the army for at least ten years. As consuls or ex-consuls, senior military commanders were also successful politicians. Popular folk-heroes were the great conquering generals: Fabius Maximus Cunctator, 'the Delayer' who had seen off Hannibal; Scipio Africanus, 'the African Victor' who had overcome Carthage; Pompey 'the Great', who had extended the Roman empire eastwards to the Euphrates; Julius Caesar, who had subjugated the Gauls.

The zenith of a Roman political career was a triumphal procession through the streets of the capital, the only time a commander could legitimately lead men under arms into Rome. In June AD 71, the emperor Vespasian and his son Titus celebrated their brutal suppression of a Jewish revolt. In late summer 70, Titus had besieged and captured Jerusalem. Herod's great Temple was sacked and its inner sanctum, the Holy of Holies, despoiled. Sacred vessels, the gold offering table, the great seven-branched candlestick (*menorah*), silver trumpets, and the scrolls of the law (*torah*) were taken back to Rome and paraded through the streets. Ten years later, in AD 81, that moment of exaltation over a vanquished people was permanently commemorated at the eastern approach to the Forum by the building of an arch dedicated to Titus (who had died earlier that year). The arch was a lasting symbol of imperial dominance; its sculptures an indelible reminder of the fate of those who rebelled against Roman rule. All who passed through unavoidably replayed this triumph; for a moment they too were at the very heart of a conquering empire: on one side flanked by the treasures from the Temple in Jerusalem, on the other by Titus himself, riding in a chariot surrounded by soldiers and escorted by personifications of Honour, Courage, and Victory.

The splendid pageantry of a triumph also told the story of the campaign. On great mobile stages 15 metres high the war was vividly represented in all its cruel detail. These painted tableaux, framed in ivory and gold, allowed an admiring holiday crowd to recapture something of the thrill of conquest, safe in the knowledge that Rome would crush its enemies. One (probably eyewitness) description is offered by the contemporary Jewish historian, Flavius Josephus, perhaps on this occasion straining his generally clear Roman sympathies.

> Here was to be seen a once prosperous countryside devastated, there entire enemy war-bands slaughtered; men fleeing and others taken into captivity ... cities whose battlements were crowded with defenders utterly overwhelmed, an army streaming in within the walls, the whole place swimming in blood, the hands of those incapable of resistance raised in supplication, temples set on fire, houses pulled down with their owners still inside, and after complete desolation and misery, rivers flowing, not through tilled fields, nor supplying drinking-water to men and animals, but through countryside still blazing on all sides.

The triumph of Vespasian and Titus, although magnificent, marked the suppression of a revolt, rather than the annexation of new territory. Even more extravagant were the spectacles of the 1st century BC, when the greatest Roman generals paraded their

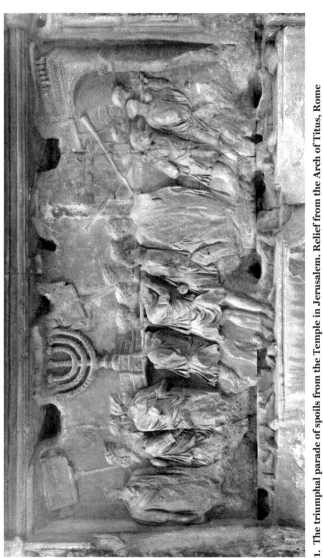

1. The triumphal parade of spoils from the Temple in Jerusalem. Relief from the Arch of Titus, Rome

conquests. In September 46, over 12 days of festivities, Julius Caesar celebrated his successes in Gaul, Africa, Egypt, and Pontus (on the southern shore of the Black Sea). This was one of the greatest triumphs ever staged. On each day there were new marvels: on one an exhibition of captives (some released, some put to death); on another a display of exotic animals (this was the first time a giraffe had been seen in Rome); on another a naval battle presented in a specially excavated lake; on another, in the Circus Maximus, captives fighting in large-scale pitched battles, one involving 40 elephants. Suspended high above their heads, silken awnings (yet another of Caesar's lavish innovations) shaded the spectators, who applauded as thousands of prisoners died. In these triumphs the killing fields of empire were re-enacted in the very heart of the capital. The cheering crowd rejoiced in the achievement of its armies and the destruction of those who opposed Rome. In the final triumph the colourful procession of painted scenes depicting Caesar's victory in Pontus was interrupted by a placard bearing a simple message. This slogan – often and wrongly associated with Caesar's brief and inconsequential campaign in Britain – was another terse reminder of Roman military superiority: *Veni, uidi, uici*, 'I came, I saw, I conquered.'

It is easy to be carried away by such rousing glorifications of conquest. Easy to forget that each triumph (over 70 were granted between 252 and 53 BC) also marked the wholesale capture and slaughter of large numbers of soldiers and civilians. It is important to pause and reflect for a moment on the sheer terror and ruthless destruction that marked the acquisition of the Roman empire. Julius Caesar's troops in Gaul killed one million enemy combatants and enslaved another million. In human and economic terms, Caesar's conquests – even allowing for the exaggeration in his own self-promoting accounts of his army's cruelty – were not to be equalled in the sheer scale of their destruction until the Spanish invasion of the Americas.

The initial brutality of conquest was matched by the overwhelming force with which any subsequent rebellions were suppressed. In AD 60 in south-eastern Britain the local population of Iceni revolted – or, perhaps better, attempted to regain their independence. Camulodunum, Verulamium, and Londinium (modern Colchester, St Albans, and London) were sacked. Roman counter-attacks swiftly re-imposed control. Thousands of Britons were killed; Roman casualties numbered barely 400. In an early example of ethnic cleansing, the Roman army continued to target the Iceni until all opposition was eliminated. Boudica, one of the Iceni leaders, took her own life. Her efforts to expel the Romans had been a miserable and costly failure.

The formidable efficiency with which the Roman army invaded and pacified enemy territory is strikingly celebrated on the 30-metre-high column dedicated in AD 113 to commemorate the emperor Trajan's two campaigns in Dacia in the previous decade. The white marble column – still standing in the centre of Rome – is decorated with a narrow band of sculpture in low relief (like an outsize cartoon strip) which spirals 24 times round the shaft. In all, 2,500 figures make up 154 recognizably separate scenes. Rather than give a straightforward account of Trajan's campaigns, these images offer the viewer a more idealized narrative of the expansion of empire. Here the Roman army appears in good marching order: energetic and disciplined legionaries construct camps, forts, roads, and bridges; they besiege and capture a hostile fortress; they are unfailingly victorious in battle. In this picture-book world there are never any Roman casualties, only the enemy is killed. Here too success is always ensured by the commanding presence of the emperor. Trajan is shown leading his troops into combat, receiving embassies, consulting his senior officers, addressing his men, and sacrificing to ensure the favour of the gods.

In the same matter-of-fact way Trajan's Column also records the atrocities of war. Defeated Dacians grovel, begging for clemency; some are imprisoned, others tortured. Villages are torched, their defenceless inhabitants butchered along with their animals.

Trophy-hunting Roman soldiers display the severed heads of their enemies to the emperor and his staff.

At the conclusion of the campaign native families and their livestock are forcibly evicted; their land now belongs to Roman settlers. The backdrop of these scenes of conquest is certainly Dacia, but the themes are universal: the inevitability of Roman supremacy, the futility of resistance, and the routine violence that accompanies the acquisition of new territories. As Trajan's Column publicly and proudly proclaimed, for those reckless enough to attempt it,

2. Troops display severed enemy heads to the emperor Trajan and his staff. Relief from Trajan's Column, Rome

these were the cruel consequences of opposing the imposition of Roman rule.

Some rebels were prepared to risk all. For those who applaud courageously futile attempts to halt the march of empire, there can be no more inspiring story than the last stand of the Jewish revolt (not finally crushed until spring AD 74, nearly four years after the sack of Jerusalem). One of the most committed Jewish sects was known as the *sicarii*, or 'dagger-men'. Members of this urban hit-squad, hiding knives beneath their cloaks and merging into the throng of pilgrims crowding Jerusalem, assassinated high-ranking Jews whom they denounced as collaborators. In summer 66, when the revolt broke out, the *sicarii* seized Masada from its Roman garrison. Masada was one of the best-defended fortresses in Judaea. Built on a narrow, sheer-sided plateau to the west of the Dead Sea, it commanded clear views high above a shimmering, salt-encrusted plain. Here the *sicarii* held out defiantly as Jerusalem fell to Titus and even after his triumph in Rome.

Against 967 men, women, and children trapped in Masada, the Roman general Flavius Silva, in charge of mopping-up operations in the subjugated province, deployed one legion and its auxiliary troops (in all, 8,000 to 9,000 men) for nearly a year. The outlines of the stone-built camps – some of the best preserved in the Roman world – are still visible on the plain, as is the four-kilometre wall that surrounded the base of the plateau. Both the camps and the wall are dwarfed by a huge assault ramp: 205 metres long, climbing 70 metres (the height of a 20-storey building) at an incline of 1 in 3. At its top was constructed a stone platform 23 metres across to serve as the base for a battering ram.

These dry statistics are impressive enough, but they can only hint at the mounting terror of the Jews who day by day watched these siege-works being inexorably raised against the fortress. Like the extravagant expenditure of a triumph which loudly proclaimed the dominance of Rome, the siege of Masada was another

3. Masada, siege ramp against the western escarpment

demonstration of the might of an empire which could concentrate extraordinary resources against even a thousand dissidents who dared oppose it. Like the Arch of Titus in far-away Rome, the great ramp, which still stands firm against Masada's western escarpment, was a permanent reminder of the impossibility of rebellion.

Faced with certain death, the *sicarii* preferred suicide. All but seven killed themselves. Two women and five children hid in the water conduits which supplied the fort from underground cisterns. It was these survivors who reported on the final hours of the last remnants of the Jewish revolt and the rallying cry of their leader, Eleazar.

> Come! While our hands are free and can hold a sword, let them serve us nobly. Let us die unenslaved by our enemies and as free men quit this life along with our wives and children. . . . Let us press on and deprive the Romans of their anticipated satisfaction at our capture, leaving them instead dumbfounded by our death and in awe of our daring.

The imperial mission

Powerful accounts of the destructive consequences of empire are rare. In their own explanations of their expansion and of subsequent measures taken to control captured provinces, the Romans seldom recognized that they had been the aggressors. Rather, wars had been fought to pacify enemies who were judged to pose a threat to the integrity of Roman territory. The acquisition of empire had been the unplanned consequence of a moderate and reasonable policy of homeland security. Cicero, the most famous orator of the 1st century BC, put the case simply and clearly: 'The only reason for waging war is so that we Romans may live in peace.'

That theme was magnificently elaborated by the poet Virgil, writing in the decade after Actium and the victory of Octavian/Augustus. The *Aeneid*, one of the greatest epic poems ever conceived, follows the fate of the Trojan prince Aeneas, fleeing the destruction of his home town at the hands of the Greeks, who on Ulysses' shrewd advice had cunningly concealed themselves in the belly of a wooden horse. Virgil's *Aeneid* picks up where Homer's *Iliad* leaves off. Aeneas escapes from Troy carrying his aged father Anchises on his back, his young son Ascanius struggling to keep up. Here begins a grand narrative which will sweep Aeneas westward across the Mediterranean, first to Carthage and finally to Italy. Here the Trojans fight the native Rutilians, who resist the attempts of these foreign invaders to seize their land. But the Rutilians are fated to fail. Their king, Turnus, falls in single combat to the victorious Aeneas. It is Aeneas' divine purpose, furthered by Jupiter, king of the Gods, to father a people destined to rule the Mediterranean world.

Virgil's *Aeneid* offers a very short introduction to Roman history. Aeneas' quest to find a new home closely prefigures Rome's mission to found an empire. At the beginning of his adventures, blown off course by a storm, he finds safe harbour in Carthage. One of the toughest tests Aeneas must undergo is to liberate himself from the voluptuous delights of this city and the manifest charms of Dido, its queen. He nearly fails. Aeneas' private Punic War is as difficult and as hard fought as Rome's. Dido is no less formidable in love than Hannibal will be in war. After a night of nuptial passion, with a thunderstorm as its suitable accompaniment, Aeneas is reminded of his destiny by Mercury, Jupiter's messenger. In a god-inspired frenzy, Aeneas orders the Trojans to set sail. Deserted and distraught, Dido commits suicide at the news, her self-destruction a foretelling of Carthage's own obliteration at the end of the Third Punic War.

Fleeing Carthage, Aeneas first makes landfall in Sicily, where he buries his father, Anchises. Then to Cumae near Naples. Deep within her cave he consults the Sibyl, the ancient seer of Apollo. At the god's command, Aeneas journeys to the Underworld to learn of his fate and the future of his loyal followers. Here, with his father's ghost as guide, he sees a procession of Roman heroes yet to be born; a triumphal parade of imperial history from Rome's beginnings through the conquest of Italy, the Punic Wars, the annexation of the eastern Mediterranean, and down to Pompey, Julius Caesar, and Augustus. In this vision Rome's destiny is revealed. As Anchises prophesies:

> Others will cast more tenderly in bronze
> Their breathing figures, I can well believe,

And bring more lifelike portraits out of marble;
Argue more eloquently, use the pointer
To trace the paths of heaven accurately
And accurately foretell the rising stars.
Roman, remember by your strength to rule
Earth's peoples – for your arts are to be these:
To pacify, to impose the rule of law,
To spare the conquered, battle down the proud.

Other people's national epics are often difficult to read without an ironic smile. In the 21st century many readers – reflecting on the problematic legacy of European colonialism – may be unwilling to endorse Virgil's poetic proclamation of Rome's imperial mission to civilize lesser breeds without the law. That said, the *Aeneid* should not be dismissed out of hand as a pacific justification for an oppressive régime. Its commentary on war and peace is more subtle than that. It is possible to feel deep sympathy for the dying Dido, loved and abandoned by Aeneas. In single combat Aeneas himself hesitates before brutally dispatching Turnus, the defeated Rutilian king. However justified Turnus' death is in terms of Aeneas' divinely sponsored quest to establish his followers and their descendants in Italy, it is still a savage act carried out in the crazed bloodlust of rage and revenge. Even so, like triumphal processions which noisily celebrated the success of a general, the purpose of the *Aeneid* was not to give the defeated an equal voice. While it did not openly glory in the slaughter of Rome's enemies (perhaps reflecting a society under Augustus glutted by three centuries of conquest and a long civil war), the *Aeneid* was clear in its positive portrayal of the Roman imperial achievement. It was intended to stand firm against much bleaker assessments.

By contrast, in his account of the final defeat of British opposition in AD 83, the contemporary historian Cornelius Tacitus gave a brilliant speech to its leader Calgacus, who (before his inevitable defeat in the face of overwhelming military force) offered a bitter critique of imperial rule. Such imaginings by Roman writers of the objections to empire are rare. They are a precious indication that not all, even amongst the victors, nodded in quiescent approval at the destruction and slaughter that conquest inevitably entailed. Against the pious justifications proposed by the *Aeneid* should be placed Calgacus' stark condemnation of Roman imperialism.

> Pillagers of the world, now they have exhausted the land by their indiscriminate devastation, they probe the sea. If their enemy is wealthy, they are greedy; if poor, they are overweening; neither East nor West has sated them . . . To plunder, slaughter, and rapine they falsely give the name 'empire'. They make a desolation and they call it 'peace'.

Like the defiant challenge of Eleazer atop Masada, some may have admired these words as the stirring sentiments of a freedom-fighter prepared to die bravely rather than surrender his independence. Yet for most, Calgacus' speech was no more than the dangerously misguided propaganda of a rebel terrorist ignorantly seeking to halt the divinely sanctioned advance of Roman rule.

Chapter 2
Imperial power

The parade of power

Tourists in the great city of Ephesus (on the Aegean coast of Turkey) might have found themselves rudely pushed aside by those eager to catch sight – or get out of the way – of an impressive procession of at least 250 priests, young men, and civic functionaries carrying 31 small statues of silver and gold. The parade was instituted in February AD 104 following a generous gift of land, money, and bullion from Caius Vibius Salutaris, one of the wealthiest men in Ephesus. Such generosity was magnificently commemorated in a lengthy inscription conspicuously displayed at the southern entrance to the city's theatre. The inscription – one of the longest surviving from anywhere in the Roman empire, 568 lines divided into 6 columns covering nearly 16 square metres of marble – set out at length Salutaris' various benefactions and recorded their grateful acceptance by his fellow-citizens. Even if they could not read the extensive detail, passers-by could still appreciate the impressive scale of this civic monument to Salutaris' munificence.

In his careful regulation of this public parade, Salutaris offered both participants and onlookers a brief guide to the history of Ephesus. The procession started outside the city at the Temple of Artemis, one of the seven wonders of the world and amongst the wealthiest shrines in the eastern Mediterranean. Ephesus was famous for its worship of Artemis. The goddess, the daughter of Zeus and Leto, had been born in a sacred grove outside the city. Here her mother had found sanctuary, safe from the jealousy of Hera, Zeus' wife. Nine statues of Artemis, eight in silver and one in gold, punctuated the procession; reminders that even in the 2nd century AD, when Ephesus had long been part of the Roman empire, it continued to value its close connection with the traditional Greek gods.

The city's ancient history was on display too. According to a long-held tradition, 1,100 years before Salutaris' benefaction Ephesus had been founded by the hero Androclus. In slaying a boar, flushed out by a grass fire started by the upsetting of a frying pan of sizzling fish, Androclus had fulfilled an oracle of Apollo that a city should be established by settlers, 'where a fish shall show them and a wild boar lead the way'. In the early 3rd century BC, Ephesus was refounded by Lysimachus, one of the close companions of Alexander the Great. Lysimachus had moved the city to its present site, facing a navigable harbour and well defended by an impressive circuit wall. In Salutaris' benefaction these significant moments in Ephesus' past were commemorated by the inclusion in the parade of silver images of the city's two founders and of Mount Pion, which rose protectively behind the commercial district of Lysimachus' new town and on whose slopes Androclus had once hunted the boar.

In all, the procession took about 90 minutes to complete its circular route, from the Temple of Artemis through the city's main streets and back again. With its 250 celebrants and 31 statues, the procession offered a working model of Ephesian society, of the city's divine connections, and of its foundation (and refoundation) long before any Roman conquest. It mattered too that this carefully choreographed *tableau vivant* seamlessly incorporated more recent events. The statue of Ephesus' town council was preceded by a personification of the Roman Senate and followed (after another of Artemis) by one representing the Roman People. Most importantly, the whole parade was headed by silver statues of the reigning emperor Trajan and his wife Plotina. These shimmering images of

Roman rule were linked directly in one long processional chain with both Ephesus' founding fathers and Artemis, its protecting deity.

By celebrating a living emperor as if he were a god, the Ephesians not only acknowledged the supremacy of imperial power, but also sought to understand and connect it to more local concerns. As this mobile history lesson processed in slow and stately rhythm through a monumental cityscape, it helped to make coherent sense of Ephesus' place in the Roman empire. In the Upper Agora, the city's newest quarter, both Trajan and Artemis were carried past temples to the deified Julius Caesar and Augustus; past a colossal statue (four times life-size) housed in a late 1st-century shrine dedicated to the 'divinely favoured emperors'. Here, above all, the procession suggested that, however far-distant Trajan might be, like other rulers before him, and like Artemis herself, he had a special concern for the city. As emperor, Trajan only visited Ephesus once (briefly in late autumn 113 en route to Antioch and the eastern frontier), but its citizens confidently asserted his ever-watchful care. Reaffirming their own importance in the vastness of empire, they paraded Trajan's glittering silver statue through the city's streets, as Salutaris' regulations demanded, once every two weeks.

A generation earlier, two of the wealthiest families in the town of Aphrodisias (about 130 kilometres up-country from Ephesus) celebrated their own importance and their city's special relationship with Rome. Together they funded the building of two splendid white marble porticoes dedicated to Aphrodite (in whose honour the town was named) and 'the divinely favoured god-emperors'. The porticoes stood three storeys high, facing each other across a broad, marble-paved road about 90 metres long. At one end stood a monumental gateway; at the other, magnificently framed, a temple dedicated to the imperial cult. Columns divided the two upper storeys of each portico into roughly square panels, 190 in all, each decorated with figured sculpture. The middle storey of the north portico carried personifications of the peoples conquered under Augustus. Directly opposite on the south portico were scenes from

Greek myth. Above, on the top storey, panels depicting emperors were placed next to those representing Olympian gods. Here historical time and eternity merged. A winged Victory separated panels celebrating Claudius' invasion of Britain in AD 43 and the temporary military success in Armenia in AD 54, at the very beginning of Nero's reign. Like the Olympian gods, these Roman emperors were represented as heroic male nudes. A well-built Augustus, his cloak dramatically billowing behind him, receives homage from figures representing the Land and the Sea. A stocky Claudius stands triumphantly over a defeated Britannia, pulling her head back by the hair, ready to strike a death blow.

These are remarkable scenes. At the same time as they celebrate Roman victory, they also seek to understand it as part of a cosmic order defined by traditional myth and ancient deities. By thinking of emperors as godlike, unconstrained by the limitations of time or distance, those in the provinces could attempt to make sense of their own subjugation. Their own non-Roman past could be linked, in a seemingly unbroken progression, with a very Roman present. In Aphrodisias, even conquest – the harshest fact of empire – was incorporated into the long-standing religious framework of the Greek world, its brutality dulled by a series of images that argued for a connection between Greek myth and Roman history, between Aphrodisias and Rome, and between Olympian gods and naked Roman emperors. Viewers of this sculptural programme were able to glory in the further advance of Roman rule. In this imperial world-view, Aphrodisias – unlike Britannia – would never lie supine at the feet of an emperor.

This basic pattern was repeated time and time again. The citizens of Mytilene (on the island of Lesbos in the north-eastern Aegean) passed a decree instituting four-yearly games in honour of Augustus and sacrifices on his birthday. The conduct of both was to be modelled on the existing cult of Zeus. The text was proudly inscribed along with the instructions given to the envoys charged with informing the emperor in person. In their speech before

4. Claudius triumphs over Britannia. Relief from the temple complex for the imperial cult, Aphrodisias

Augustus, they were to emphasize that the Mytileneans recognized that their proposals were of little importance to those 'who have attained heavenly glory and possess the pre-eminence and power of the gods'; but they were also to make it clear that, if any additional honours for the emperor could be devised, they would be immediately instituted, since 'the enthusiasm and devotion of the city will not fall short in anything which can make him even more of a god'.

Far away on the other side of the Mediterranean, leading members of communities in Gaul set up inscriptions in honour of such strange, hybrid deities as Nemausus Augustus, Bormana Augusta, Mars Loucetius Augustus, Augustus Deus Anuallus, or the Comedouae Augustae. Like the presence of Artemis and Trajan in Salutaris' parade in Ephesus, or the association of Zeus and Augustus in Mytilene, this explicit joining of ancestral gods and Roman emperors again demonstrated the dynamic capacity of traditional systems of belief to respond creatively in finding new ways to understand the nature of conquest. A form of 'religious bilingualism' helped fuse imperial and local concerns.

In Gaul too, as throughout the empire, emperor-worship was often a matter of hotly contested social prestige. In the late 170s, the emperors Marcus Aurelius and Commodus intervened to prevent the costs of the priesthood at Lugdunum (modern Lyon in southern France), the centre of the imperial cult in Gaul, escalating further through the rivalry of its incumbents. Each sought to outdo the last by the provision of ever more lavish gladiatorial games. A decree issued by the Senate in Rome set maximum prices for gladiators and capped the charges levied by their trainers. The desire for a glorious public display to celebrate the divinity of the emperor had to be balanced against the need to ensure that the imperial priesthood should not become prohibitively expensive. It was important to all concerned that one of the most prestigious offices in the province should remain a highly prized post for the wealthiest members of the Gallic elite.

In the city of Rome the focus of the imperial cult was firmly on the divinity of deceased emperors. Surrounding the Forum, their imposing temples and monuments dominated the political and religious centre of empire. The earliest temple, dedicated to the deified Julius Caesar, was commissioned by his supporters in 42 BC, two years after his assassination. Caesar's divinity had been confirmed by the appearance of a comet which signalled the advent of a new god in the heavens. For Octavian, Caesar's adopted son, this justified his own evocative self-description as *diui filius* – 'son of a god'. In the ensuing civil wars this startling epithet emphasized his divine favour. It also offered one explanation for his victory. For the defeated Mark Antony, Octavian was 'the youth who owed everything to his name'. Augustus' own divinity was signalled by the release from the top of his funeral pyre of an eagle, the bird sacred to Jupiter, king of the gods. At times such wondrous moments of apotheosis (in as much as they could ever be faithfully represented) might require more elaborate imagining. A relief on the base of a column erected shortly after AD 161 to honour the recently deceased emperor Antoninus Pius showed both the emperor and his wife Faustina (who had died 20 years earlier) carried heavenwards on the back of a splendidly winged youth. Flanked by eagles, they soar high above personifications of the city of Rome.

5. **Apotheosis of Antoninus Pius and Faustina. Relief from the base of Column of Antoninus Pius, Rome, now in the Vatican Museums**

Modern viewers sometimes stare at such arresting images with blank incredulity. For many it can be difficult to comprehend a religious system that does not recognize an impermeable barrier between humanity and divinity. In the ancient world, these were not clearly delimited polar opposites. What mattered was not so much an individual's nature (as human or divine), but rather his or her status within a blurred spectrum of intermediate possibilities. It can also be difficult to conceive of a society with no firm division between religion and politics. Yet in the Roman empire, the religious rituals surrounding emperor-worship were not somehow secondary to the 'real business' of rule (administration, justice, taxation, warfare). Rather, religious imagery and religious language were an inseparable part of Roman political vocabulary.

For its enthusiasts, the worship of living emperors and their posthumous deification offered a means of understanding what it meant to be part of the Roman empire. It could connect individuals and communities, whether in Ephesus, Aphrodisias, Mytilene, or Gaul, to a single imperial centre. It could integrate traditional gods and long-standing local beliefs within a ritual framework reduplicated across the whole Mediterranean. It could provide a language for comprehending absolute power. For wealthy men like Caius Vibius Salutaris, supreme in their own communities, to be seen to bow in obeisance to another human being would be to risk unthinkable social humiliation; but to worship a god offered local grandees a way of recognizing their inferiority without any loss of face. Indeed, in the competition for civic and personal glory, the celebration of a special connection with a superhuman emperor both reinforced the privileged position of those who held priesthoods, funded festivals, or paid for the construction of temples, and confirmed the superior status of their cities. Above all, it openly paraded their membership of a world-wide imperial society. A fragmentary list of proverbial questions and answers preserved on a scrap of papyrus from 2nd-century Egypt succinctly sums up such an attractive view of the hierarchies imposed by empire – on both heaven and earth.

> What is a god? The exercise of power.
> What is a ruler? Like a god.

The problems of proximity

For many close to the imperial centre, and particularly those at court, such confident proclamations of divinity did not always adequately capture the complexities of dealing with emperors face to face. After all, there is an obvious distance between the empress Faustina standing demurely at her loving husband's side as they are both serenely transported to heaven, and the rumours of a headstrong women whose loose living was restrained by Antoninus Pius' strict domestic discipline. Likewise, there is an obvious distance between the heroically nude and strikingly well-proportioned Claudius on the south portico at Aphrodisias and the stammering, dribbling, weak-kneed emperor who as a boy was said to have been unfeelingly dismissed by his mother Antonia as not fully human: 'not so much unfinished by nature, as barely begun'.

This dissonance between autocracy – godlike in its exercise of absolute power – and the all too mortal failings of those who ruled the Roman empire might at times, and understandably, provoke some amusement. The best wisecracks were made by emperors themselves. On his deathbed in June 79, Vespasian was reported to have quipped sardonically, 'Damn it, I think I'm becoming a god!' Twenty-five years earlier, in AD 54, Lucius Annaeus Seneca (the famous moralist, philosopher, and playwright) had written a biting satire on the deification of the emperor Claudius. Its title, *Apocolocyntosis* – a neat word-play on the Greek 'apotheosis' – is roughly translatable into English as *Pumpkin-ification*. Seneca imagined the deceased Claudius standing on the celestial threshold of Olympus loudly demanding admission. Somewhat taken aback, Jupiter put the request to the assembled divinities. The debate concluded with a long speech from Claudius' great-uncle, the deified Augustus, who vigorously opposed the motion. 'Was it for this that I secured peace both on land and sea? Was it for this that I curbed civil wars? . . . Who will worship this man as a god? Who will believe in him? As long as you make gods of this sort, no one will believe that you are gods yourselves.' All present agreed. Claudius was summarily ejected from heaven and dragged down by Mercury to eternal punishment in the Underworld.

For all their biting wit, such humorous burlesques should be taken seriously. They are not so much evidence of a kind of cynical scepticism towards imperial divinity on the part of the Roman elite, as a recognition (as is often the case with the best political satire in our own society) both of the difficulties in comprehending power and of the anxieties surrounding any direct criticism of its exercise. The problem was less one of accepting the authority of a living emperor, than of constructing a moral framework which might enable imperial actions to be judged. In his philosophical treatise *On Mercy* (written within two years of *Pumpkin-ification*, and addressed to the emperor Nero), Seneca argued that the exercise of imperial power also imposed its own constraints. Those responsible for keeping the peace had always to be prepared to go to war. Those responsible for justice had always to check their emotions and their language.

> You may think it hard that monarchs should be deprived of that freedom of speech which even the humblest enjoy. 'This is slavery,' you may say, 'not supreme power.' Really? Are you not aware that supreme power means noble slavery for you? . . . The slavery of being supremely great lies in the impossibility of ever becoming anything less. This restraint you have in common with the gods. They too are held tightly bound to the heavens . . . you too are fixed to your pinnacle.

That emperors, although godlike in their possession of imperial power, might also be bound by a moral code which could reasonably be expected to govern their behaviour was an insistent theme in the praises offered by the aristocratic elite. In Rome in September 100, the distinguished senator Pliny the Younger delivered a speech before Trajan and the Senate thanking the emperor for the award of a consulship. In his panegyric Pliny was keen to emphasize Trajan's cardinal virtues: clemency, simplicity, piety, liberality, accessibility. In his concern for justice he was like a god, 'who sees all, hears all, and wherever his aid is invoked is present in a moment'. Indeed, even Jupiter had reason to be grateful: 'he has so much time free for the heavens now that he has given you to us to discharge his duties towards the whole human race'. Above all, Pliny praised Trajan for his *ciuilitas*: for his behaviour as a citizen amongst citizens collectively bound by the rule of law and a mutual respect for social status. In Pliny's carefully constructed political economy, a good king was also a good citizen – a paradox frequently restated with artful rhetorical brilliance. Indeed, in the sheer epigrammatic dazzle of Pliny's words, it is almost possible to forget that a monarch cannot also be a subject.

> The emperor is one of us, and his superiority is greater and more conspicuous because he thinks of himself as one of us, and bears in mind that he is a man just as much as a ruler over men. . . . For when a man can advance no further than the highest rank, the only way he can go even higher is by stepping down.

It is never easy to praise an autocrat to his face. Pliny's elegant rhetorical formulations capture – if just for a moment – something of the difficulties faced by courtiers who knew Trajan personally and depended for their success on his continuing goodwill. It was not a simple matter to make coherent sense of the range of possible, and at times clearly conflicting, ways of understanding imperial power. For Pliny, what was at stake (as in Ephesus or Aphrodisias) was the assertion of some connection between his audience and the emperor. At its core, his speech was an argument for a community of interest between Trajan and the empire's elite. It was this group's privileges that a praiseworthy emperor should seek to protect, displaying, in Pliny's view, no greater virtue than a willingness to be seen as 'one of us'. Indeed, it was Trajan's very behaviour as a citizen that (in another memorable paradox) secured his supremacy: 'For you are raised to the heavens by the very ground on which we all tread and where the footprints of an emperor are mingled with our own.'

Writing imperial power

Many of the expectations implicit in Pliny's praises of Trajan's exercise of imperial power are more openly on display in a series of imperial biographies written by his contemporary and protégé Suetonius, a scholar and able administrator who held a series of important court posts under Trajan and his successor Hadrian. Like Pliny, Suetonius was explicit in his moral judgements. He offered both praise and condemnation, the latter possible at a suitable distance. All of his imperial subjects were safely dead: Domitian, the last emperor in the *Lives of the Caesars*, died a generation before Suetonius wrote.

As a biographer, Suetonius aimed above all to reveal the secret springs of human action. Good emperors could be distinguished by their virtues: liberality, *ciuilitas*, moderation, clemency. Their personal merits and well-regulated private lives mirrored a political programme which respected the position and importance of the wealthy elite in Rome. In Suetonius' view, Augustus, the paradigm of excellence, had restored the prestige of the Senate and recognized its pre-eminence. As he had brought order to the state, so Augustus' private life was also an admirable model of self-restraint.

> His lack of expense on furniture and household goods may be seen from the couches and tables which are still in existence . . . They say that he did not sleep on any bed unless it was low and plainly furnished . . . He was a frugal eater (for I would not even omit this detail) and usually ate simple fare. He was especially fond of coarse bread, whitebait, handmade soft cheese, and green figs.

Bad emperors were marked out by their vices: pride, cruelty, avarice, luxury, lust. The defects in their characters and the disorderly excess of their private lives mirrored a culpable lack of concern with maintaining Rome's social hierarchy. For Suetonius, Caligula's shameless courting of public popularity amongst ordinary citizens was certain evidence of the disintegration of a proper order. His threat to award a consulship to his favourite horse was not to be seen as a well-turned and deliberate insult to the office at the apex of a successful senatorial career, but rather as an indication of an equine obsession bordering on madness. In this topsy-turvy world, an emperor who in public was alleged to break all the bounds of decency by ordering senators to run alongside his chariot, could also be believed in private to indulge in extravagant banquets and extraordinary sexual exploits with men, women, the wives of senators, and even his own sisters.

The same morally degenerative pattern observed by Suetonius in Caligula was repeated in his successor Nero. Nero was to be blamed for the great fire in Rome in AD 64. It was the prelude to a cynical land grab. On a 50-hectare site in the centre of the city the emperor constructed a new palace in beautifully landscaped pleasure gardens. In its extent and luxury, Nero's 'Golden House' far exceeded the imperial residences built by Augustus and successors on the Palatine Hill overlooking the Forum. In Suetonius' view, the creation of what amounted to a country estate in the heart of Rome was a perversion of the natural order of things: an all too visible sign of a régime that had no interest in the maintenance of a well-regulated society. The threat that imperial power might rest more on mass appeal in the city than elite support in the Senate was most wantonly on display in Nero's enthusiasm for popular pastimes such as chariot racing, plays, and gladiatorial games. For Suetonius, this was certain proof of a fatally flawed character. The moral lesson was clear. An emperor who fought in the arena and appeared on stage could more plausibly be condemned as a dangerous egomaniac strumming a lyre and singing a Homeric ditty as the capital of the world went up in flames.

A close concern with Nero's dramatic abilities is also the dominant theme in the most influential account of his reign, and one which, along with Suetonius' biographies, has done much to shape modern perceptions of Roman emperors. Cornelius Tacitus – a contemporary of both Pliny and Suetonius – is one of the most subtle historians and sophisticated political commentators whose works survive from Antiquity. In his *Annals* (completed some time around 120), Tacitus presented Nero's willingness to act out a variety of roles on stage as a public expression of a set of skills continually rehearsed in the more private world of the imperial palace. Here too the emperor performed. Here too a small audience of courtiers and the imperial family tried to second-guess the plot in order to know when to applaud, when to speak, and when to remain silent.

One of the most memorable scenes in the *Annals* opens with the imperial household dining together in a seemingly convincing picture of familial conviviality. Amongst the company was Agrippina, Nero's mother, as well as the young Octavia and her brother Britannicus, who as the last surviving son of the emperor Claudius represented the most serious dynastic threat to Nero's imperial position. During the dinner, Britannicus collapsed. Speechless, he fell to the floor desperately gasping for breath. This (at least in Tacitus' account) is a murder scene. A hot drink, already tasted by Britannicus' attendant, had been cooled by water containing a fatal poison. As the young prince expired, Nero observed that nothing unusual was happening. The boy was epileptic and would soon recover. As it became clear that Britannicus was not acting up – but was actually dead – those less practised in the artifices of court etiquette hurriedly left the room. The more adept stayed in their places. Britannicus' loving sister Octavia did not flinch (to quote Tacitus): 'despite her youthful inexperience, she had learned to conceal her grief, her affection, her every feeling'. All kept their gaze fixed on Nero and followed his lead. 'And so after this brief silence, the festive pleasures of the meal were resumed.'

Nero's court is a dangerous world in which even silent observers, like the innocent Octavia, collude in disguising their real feelings. In March 59, four years after Britannicus' death, Nero invited his mother to holiday with him at Baiae on the fashionable Campanian coast near modern Naples. Agrippina agreed, genuinely expecting (according to Tacitus) to enjoy herself. Moreover, Nero had ordered a new and lavishly appointed boat to convey her across the bay following a banquet at which he had been particularly attentive and loving. On a bright starlit night, not far from shore, disaster struck. All seemed to go as Nero planned: the boat collapsed – as perhaps it had really been designed to do. This was to be another murder. But Agrippina and her maid Acerronia, saved by the stout sides of the couches on which they were reclining, were not crushed to death. In the confusion that followed, they were pitched into the water.

Acerronia, thinking that it would help her to be rescued, shouted that she was Agrippina. But her acting was too good; the crew beat her to death with boat hooks and oars. Agrippina herself remained silent and, only slightly wounded, made it safely to shore. Despite suspecting the attempt on her life, Agrippina at once sent her trusted servant Agermus to announce to Nero that she had narrowly survived an accident. The emperor in panic threw a sword at Agermus' feet and proclaimed that he had narrowly avoided assassination. Troops were sent to kill Agrippina who had, so the emperor alleged, clearly intended the death of her own son. Those at court wondered how to react to the news. Some celebrated the emperor's good fortune. But Nero himself went tearfully into mourning for the death of his mother.

In Tacitus' *Annals*, Nero's exercise of imperial power fatally deforms his world. Under Nero Rome is a dark and treacherous place where things are never quite what they seem; a place where those involved can only try to predict the emperor's whims. All – some knowingly, some accidentally, some unwillingly – are inescapably trapped in a web of dissimulation and deceit. Tacitus' central image of the political world as a stage, on which all perform and few (if any) write their own script, is seductive. For confirmed cynics or ardent republicans, this is an admonitory vision of the corrosive effects of autocracy. The *Annals* are an unremitting exposé of an imperial system which not only corrupts the powerful, but poisons the very processes of government itself. Here there can be no heroes. The attempt of Seneca (one of Nero's close advisers and author of *Apocolocyntosis* and *On Mercy*) to free himself from the unacceptable demands of the régime by committing suicide in the privacy of his own bath house is inevitably a gesture of impotent futility. For Tacitus, this pointless death presents a faintly farcical scene, cruelly exposing (as the expiring *érudit* continues to dictate his thoughts to his scribes) Seneca's exaggerated view of his own importance.

> Seneca, since his body, old and emaciated by his frugal way of living, only allowed his blood to issue slowly, severed the arteries both in his leg and behind the knee. . . . Yet even in these final moments he retained his eloquence; so he summoned his secretaries and dictated a lengthy treatise.

But for all Tacitus' attractive moralizing on the inescapable terrors of autocracy, we should be careful of being completely taken in. Through his magnificent prose, Tacitus (like the very best of 19th-century novelists) can sometimes make his readers forget that he simply could not have known many of the actions or motives which he presents as undisputed fact. If Nero, or Octavia, or Agrippina were indeed concealing their emotions, it is difficult to see how Tacitus or his sources could have known how they really felt. Rather, in Tacitus' version of imperial history, all is cunningly contrived; all carefully pre-scripted; all skilfully acted out. There is no room for a genuinely cheering crowd; no room for any real support – aristocratic, popular, or provincial. No room for wondering whether Britannicus died as the result of an epileptic fit, or if Agrippina was actually involved in a freak boating accident. Sixty years after the event, when Tacitus was writing, how could the important details of the attempted murder of Agrippina (if that's what it really was) have been gathered, or researched, or checked? How can we be confident that Tacitus could securely sift fiction from fact, even if we assume that this was invariably his intention?

Of course, other versions of Nero may be equally as convincing or as implausible – or as ultimately unknowable – as the one offered by Tacitus. But it may be possible to find other ways of thinking about the emperor's reputation. At the very least, we should start by questioning the suffocating self-sufficiency of Tacitus' account of Roman emperors, or the attractiveness of the moral templates imposed by Suetonius on his imperial biographies. Both Suetonius (always keen to assert the continued importance of the pretensions and prejudices of the Roman elite) and Tacitus (for whom power tends inevitably to corrupt) are themselves part of a debate about how imperial power should be conceived. Simply because they may seem at times to appeal more directly to modern sensibilities, this does not of itself make their accounts more accurate or credible. Both have their own artful agendas of which their readers should be acutely and uncomfortably aware.

Alongside these versions of Roman emperors we might instead seek to set a range of other views – some conflicting, some complementary, some overlapping. Next to the cool literary histories of Tacitus and Suetonius, we should set extravagant processions, expensive sculptured panels, grandiloquent speeches, and impressive inscriptions. In so doing we might not get any nearer to 'the real Nero' or to any other emperor. (In the end, this is not about judging the plausibility of one account against another.) But we might come closer to appreciating the variety of ways in which imperial power was understood and represented in the Roman world.

In mid 1st-century Aphrodisias, those responsible for the sculptural programme in the two porticoes fronting the temple to the imperial cult commissioned two marble panels in honour of Nero. Like the images of other Roman emperors, these were part of an extensive scheme which included heroes from Greek mythology and the Olympian gods. In one panel, Nero stands naked and victorious, exalting over an exhausted woman, the personification of a conquered Armenia. In the second, he wears full military dress,

6. Nero and Agrippina. Relief from the temple complex for the imperial cult, Aphrodisias

holds a spear and probably an orb, and is crowned with a laurel wreath by his mother Agrippina, who holds in her left hand a cornucopia (a horn of plenty overspilling with grapes and pomegranates). These are arresting visions of a powerful, godlike emperor. They are open celebrations of the continued might and prosperity of the Roman empire. As images of imperial power these two panels should not be too hastily dismissed – even if a historian like Tacitus might only glance at them with a wry, ironic smile.

Chapter 3
Collusion

Ruling the Roman empire

At the beginning of the 2nd century AD, a decade after he had offered a subtle and complex speech of thanks for his consulship, Pliny the Younger was sent by the emperor Trajan to govern the province of Bithynia-Pontus on the southern shore of the Black Sea. Pliny's surviving correspondence with the emperor offers an unparalleled insight into the activities of one high-ranking Roman administrator. In his letters home, Pliny advertised his zeal in carrying out his mandate. Over a two-year period he contacted Trajan 61 times on a wide range of issues, in 39 cases submitting matters for decision or approval. Pliny refrained, for example, from examining the municipal accounts of the city of Apamea, despite the citizens' willingness to make them available, until he had received an imperial warrant. (Pliny's hesitation was justifiable given that previous emperors had confirmed Apamea's exemption from an audit by the governor.) He also sought Trajan's approval for all new building works, since those undertaken in the previous decade had been a prime cause of civic over-expenditure. He reported on the failure to complete two aqueducts at Nicomedia, on subsidence in a half-built theatre at Nicaea, and on an over-ambitious scheme to construct new baths at Claudiopolis. At Nicomedia he recommended a canal, at Sinope an aqueduct, at Prusa new baths, and at Amastris the covering of a foul-smelling open sewer in the town's main street.

From one point of view, Pliny's administrative activity in Bithynia-Pontus, though no doubt necessary, seems rather banal (indeed, hardly meriting publication). That he should insist on reviewing records of civic expenditure, or seek Trajan's approval for any construction projects, or attempt to reconcile ambiguities in imperial rulings was no doubt evidence of the diligent discharge of his commission. Equally, that a governor should be concerned with the financial integrity of cities in a prosperous province might be thought uncontroversial. To modern sensibilities 39 queries directed to an emperor over a two-year period (even as a published selection from a larger set) hardly makes Pliny's governorship strikingly interventionist. But for contemporaries these detailed investigations were noteworthy precisely because they represented an intensification of standard practice. They exceeded the expected norms of Roman imperial government.

Pliny was the exception, not the rule. For the most part, Roman governors were reactive, not proactive. They did not interfere in the internal affairs of cities in their provinces. If presented with a petition or a judicial matter they might choose to adjudicate, although in many cases the decision might be no more than a referral to a local civic official. They responded to situations or disputes as requested or obliged. They were authorities to whom locals might appeal, rather than investigating magistrates acting on their own initiative. A provincial governor's restricted remit was reflected in the small number of his subordinates. It is unlikely that Pliny was able to rely on more than 100 trained bureaucrats to help him carry out his duties in Bithynia-Pontus. Militarized frontier provinces, where the possibility of revolt or attack demanded greater vigilance, provided larger staffs. In the 2nd century, the governor of Britain, a province garrisoned with three legions, was assisted by up to 450 officials, mostly seconded soldiers. Altogether across the empire, those like Pliny in charge of Roman provincial administration were supported by a total of roughly 10,000 bureaucrats.

This is a tiny number, especially to those accustomed to the close regulation imposed by modern states with their far-reaching policies and programmes. To give some crude sense of scale: to service a population roughly the same as that of the Roman empire, the British government currently employs around half a million bureaucrats. That said, Roman government never attempted (nor thought it necessary or desirable) to provide mass education, housing, health, or social security. Even so, from an administrative point of view, Roman rule over the Mediterranean world represents a magnificent economy of effort. The Roman empire can hardly be said to have been over-governed.

Small-town society

This minimalist state of affairs was one which many in the provinces were eager to preserve. Ten years before Pliny's governorship, one of the leading citizens of Prusa, a middling town in Bithynia-Pontus, appealed to his peers not to do anything which might threaten such an advantageous arrangement. Amongst the 80 surviving speeches of the accomplished orator and philosopher Dio Cocceianus – known to admiring posterity as Dio Chrysostom, 'the Golden-Mouthed' – are a number delivered before the town's assembly. Prusa (as Pliny's investigations into its baths confirmed) was an unremarkable place, much like hundreds of other towns scattered across the Mediterranean. It was attractively sited on a broad terrace below Mount Olympus, the highest peak in Bithynia. Prusa's prosperity was based on exporting timber from the heavily forested lower slopes of the mountain, on farming the wide, fertile valley which spread out below, and on attracting tourists to its thermal springs.

The inhabitants of Prusa and its surrounding territory were

represented by an assembly and a town council. The assembly was open to all adult male citizens who satisfied a minimum property qualification. Membership of the council was much more restrictive, confined to perhaps 200 or 300 of the wealthiest citizens who had held one of the city's senior official posts. These were Prusa's landed gentry; a well-off group whose income was mostly derived from their estates. Taken together, these prosperous men and their families represented the town's 'quality'. They expected their elevated position in society to be recognized and valued by all. A snobbish, self-regarding, and inward-looking set, they watched each other jealously in a continuous and hard-fought battle for status. Time was spent in a carefully organized round of engagements (dinner-parties, hunting, the performance of public duties), in the studied exercise of elaborate social etiquette, and in the slow and intricate manoeuvring which characterizes any small, privileged group tightly bound by the twin concerns of inheritance and marriage.

From the adult males of this municipal 'upper crust' the town's officials were elected annually (nominally by the assembly, but from a slate pre-selected by the council). The most senior posts were dominated by a few influential families. Both Dio Chrysostom and his son held the office of chief magistrate. Under the supervision of the council a system of local rents, indirect taxes (such as customs duties), and special levies provided funds for the running of the city: the provision of a police force, the supervision of the grain supply to ensure the availability of reasonably priced bread, the maintenance of the sewage system, the upkeep of public buildings and streets, the supply of fuel for the public baths, the regulation of private construction, and the control of weights and measures. In addition, the council's wealthiest members, as part of an endless competition for social superiority, were expected to draw on their own private resources to cover the costs of public entertainment (religious festivals, commemorative feasts, cultural and athletic contests, gladiatorial games) and to finance grand projects for the beautification of their native city.

Significantly too, the town council was collectively responsible for the payment to Rome of an annual tribute assessed in part as a poll-tax and in part on property, for organizing and supplying labour where needed (for example, for road maintenance), and for providing recruits for the army. In return for fulfilling these basic demands of empire, cities such as Prusa were permitted to manage their own internal affairs. For Dio Chrysostom, it was this freedom from imperial interference that underpinned the continued vitality of small-town society. Equally, it was the presence of empire (and the threat of reprisals in case of instability) that buttressed the superior position of the wealthy and justified their control of the city's administration.

These were significant advantages which local elites were reluctant to surrender. In the 70s AD, a crowd in Prusa, angry at the rising price of bread, demanded that Dio should be made commissioner for the grain supply and that he should use his own wealth to benefit all by subsidizing purchases on the open market. In the face of Dio's refusal, the situation turned nasty. A mob was narrowly prevented from setting fire to his house. Later, speaking before the town's assembly, Dio defended his position. He pointed to his previous benefactions and those of generations of his family, citing his grandfather who had 'spent in munificence all the fortune he had inherited from his father and grandfather, until he had nothing left'. Dio claimed to have shouldered more than his fair share of public expenditure, nor, he alleged, was he amongst the wealthiest in Prusa. He recommended that the assembly move to elect suitable grain commissioners from those who had not yet put their private fortunes to public use.

This was a double rebuke: both to the citizenry to cease pressing its claims through violence and to his fellow-councillors who, Dio pointedly observed, were collectively responsible for ensuring that Prusa was properly governed. Perhaps not everyone believed Dio's claims to modest means or the stories of his grandfather's bankrupting liberality. Even so, whatever the reluctance of the town's elite in this instance to seize the opportunity for public-spirited generosity, such unwillingness was not to their long-term advantage. To fail in this joint enterprise was to risk the unwelcome intervention of the Roman authorities. Dio underlined the point with an unflattering comparison.

> Nothing which happens in the cities goes unnoticed by the governors; on the contrary, just as the families of children who have been naughty at home report them to their teachers, so the misbehaviour of the assembly is reported to them.

Dio Chrysostom's concerns and self-interests were repeatedly echoed. In the mid 2nd century, Aelius Aristides, another famous Greek orator, delivered a panegyric in exuberant praise of Rome. Aristides' approbation was firmly grounded in his experience of local politics in Smyrna (modern Izmir on the Aegean coast of Turkey). For Aristides, what marked out the Roman empire as exceptional was its welcome lack of interest in regulating the day-to-day affairs of local communities. Not only were there few imperial officials, but away from the frontiers there were also small numbers of soldiers. In the most peaceful regions of the empire such as Asia Minor, there might be no more than 500 troops garrisoned in a whole province. Of course, large forces could quickly be called in, but importantly in towns across the Mediterranean the permanent presence of armed troops was not part of the machinery of Roman rule. Aelius Aristides was unstinting in his enthusiastic affirmation of the benefits of such a system. In his view, the empire was best described as 'a commonwealth of independent cities'. In turn, that autonomy relieved both Roman administration and the army of a considerable burden: 'There is no need to have troops stationed at strategic points in the towns, since the most eminent and powerful people in each place guard their homeland for you.'

Local elites were key to the Roman empire's success. For those who survived the initial trauma of conquest and had abandoned as hopeless any organized form of resistance, the advantages of being in a right relationship with the ruling power were all too self-evident. Indeed, for many in the provinces Roman dominance was most felt in its strengthening of the ability of existing oligarchic cliques to exercise unrivalled control in their localities. In towns like Prusa and Smyrna, the presence of empire explicitly underwrote the suffocating monopoly over the city's affairs of a small group of well-off families. And as Dio Chrysostom stressed, that was not a position which could sensibly be jeopardized by allowing civic in-fighting to disrupt public order. Similarly, in the western provinces, effective Roman government depended on an intimate relationship with local strongmen. In Spain, Gaul, and Britain, the imposition of empire brought to an end a debilitating cycle of tribal warfare and the rise and fall of leaders whose precarious position was challenged by continual conflict. Those chieftains who supported Roman rule found their status as the most prominent people in their region (after the Roman governor) reinforced by their close connection with the might of empire. They were now more secure in the possession of their power and wealth than they had ever been before the Roman conquest.

Throughout the cities of the Mediterranean world Roman rule shored up local elites. It guaranteed their importance and their authority. Even the most irksome of imperial demands, the annual payment of tribute, could be turned to advantage. Those on town councils who undertook the financial risk involved in collection were also best placed to shift the burden of payment. That might most profitably be achieved by a collusively low valuation on their own property, early demands for other people's taxes, and late payment of their own. For these notables the pressures of imperial government were both a potential source of gain and the basis of their local power. The needs of empire legitimized the sometimes violent extraction of often meagre surpluses from smallholders. On the estates of the wealthy, peasant farmers were doubly bound, both as tenants and taxpayers.

The superior position of those who ruled their localities and ensured the maintenance of peace and the regular flow of revenue was further strengthened by a grant of Roman citizenship. Citizenship was routinely conferred on the families and direct descendants of those who had held high municipal office. It was also regularly granted to soldiers in auxiliary units in the Roman army if on discharge they had completed twenty-five years of service. It was one of Dio Chrysostom's chief claims to be recognized as an influential figure in Prusa that both his mother and father were Roman citizens. The practical benefits for men like Dio were clear. They gained access to the protection offered by Roman law, and, for the wealthiest and most ambitious, to high-ranking positions in the imperial administration or army.

The prospect of citizenship also helped ensure that the ruling elites in the mosaic of towns which together made up the empire would seek to reconcile local and imperial loyalties. In 168–169 the emperors Marcus Aurelius and Lucius Verus conferred citizenship on the family of Julianus, one of the leaders of the Zegrenses, an ethnic group living high up in the Atlas Mountains in Morocco. To advertise his status as part of an empire-wide elite who enjoyed a privileged, special relationship with Rome, Julianus' eldest son (who secured citizenship for his own family nine years later) had both imperial grants permanently displayed in Latin on a finely engraved bronze plaque. For those who wished to emulate such success (and the emperors were eager to encourage others) the message was clear. Julianus, his wife, and four children had become citizens 'because he had been most loyal in his ready obedience to our side'. And in this case 'our side' – as everyone who knew Julianus was no doubt well aware – meant the Roman empire.

The possession of Roman citizenship publicly marked out a group who together could fairly claim full membership of a coherent Mediterranean-wide community of mutually convergent interests. In extending its citizenship the Roman empire was strikingly more generous than other ancient – and many modern – states. (In democratic Athens of the 5th century BC, for example, only those with both a citizen mother and father could themselves be classed as citizens.) This comparatively open-handed inclusion of local notables was a significant aspect of Roman rule singled out by Aelius Aristides for especial commendation: 'There is that thing which, much more than all other things, deserves attention and admiration: I mean your citizenship, and its grand conception, because there is nothing like it to be found anywhere else at all.' Coming from a member of that tiny, wealthy minority which enjoyed the advantages of citizenship, Aristides' praise is easily understandable. Most importantly, his enthusiasms capture one of the most enduring aspects of Roman domination: that throughout the Mediterranean world subjugated provincial elites were swiftly and successfully transformed into the empire's ruling class. Conquerors and conquered could now both describe themselves as Roman.

The monumental urge

The most visible celebration of security and prosperity in the provinces was the extensive programme of monumental building undertaken at private expense. There was hardly a city which did not benefit from the competitive urge amongst local notables to give concrete expression both to their superior position in their own municipal society and to their status as part of an imperial elite. The porticoes, libraries, temples, arches, baths, and theatres most often admired by modern visitors are in many cases the result of this self-serving upsurge in public generosity and the often extravagant desire by the wealthy to mark out their city as fully part of an empire of cities. Today, often stripped of their fine marble cladding, their brightly painted decoration forever faded, the weather-worn shells of these buildings can only gesture at their former magnificence.

In the mid 2nd century AD, Lucius Cosinius Primus, one of the leading citizens of Cuicul (modern Djemila in Algeria), funded the building of a splendid new market place. A rectangular portico (24 by 22 metres) enclosed a square containing a hexagonal, colonnaded pavilion 5 metres in diameter. An inscription that ran around the top of the portico made the extent of Cosinius' generosity absolutely clear: he had paid for, and instructed his brother Caius to oversee, the construction of 'the market place with its columns and statues . . . and pavilion'.

Importantly too, this design was self-consciously imitative. Lucius Cosinius' new market place reproduced in miniature the Great Market in Rome, completed in AD 59 and reconstructed under the emperor Nero after the fire of 64 which had destroyed large areas of the city. The Great Market consisted of a large, open square enclosed by a two-storey portico; at its centre stood an equally grand circular pavilion. This was a design repeated across the empire. To build a market place modelled on the Great Market in Rome was evidence of a close connection with metropolitan fashion. In a distant provincial town it advertised a knowledge both of the imperial capital and of an international style.

In Rome itself the Great Market was built to surpass a much older building (probably also burned down in AD 64) originally commissioned in the early 2nd century BC by Marcus Fulvius Nobilior, consul and successful general, to the ground-plan which was to become standard: a rectangular enclosure with a pavilion at its centre. This Roman original was copied in the town of Lepcis Magna (on the coast of modern Libya). Here a colonnaded piazza had at its centre two circular pavilions of fine grey limestone, each surrounded by an octagonal portico. The dedicatory inscription marking the end of building work in 8 BC linked the donor, Annobal Tapapius Rufus, with the ruling emperor, Augustus.

Rufus was also responsible for funding Lepcis Magna's magnificent new theatre. The arc of seats, 95 metres in diameter, rested in part on a natural slope, in part on a compacted fill of earth and rubble, and in part on stone-faced concrete vaults. This was an impressive achievement. Rufus paraded his generosity in a number of

7. **Market place, Lepcis Magna**

prominently placed inscriptions, two cemented in above the main doors onto the stage in full view of the audience. The text was in both Latin and Punic (the local language), the former emphasizing his connections with a wider Roman world, the latter ensuring that even those without Latin could learn of his munificence and applaud Annobal Rufus, ORNATOR PATRIAE AMATOR CONCORDIAE – 'embellisher of his home town, lover of consensus'.

Here in the theatre, the local elite could put themselves on show. Over the next century and a half, the wealthy of Lepcis Magna competed to outdo Rufus by funding ever more splendid additions:

8. Inscription honouring Annobal Rufus, theatre, Lepcis Magna

improvements to the seating with a parapet screening the chairs of the town council from the rest of the audience, a small shrine in the middle of the uppermost tier of the auditorium, and, at the rear of the stage, a magnificent ornamental marble screen standing three storeys high and decorated with over a hundred statues of divinities and members of the imperial family.

This paradigm of munificence and display was repeated again and again. Half a Mediterranean world away in Apamea (in western Syria), Lucius Julius Agrippa proclaimed his generosity to the city following a serious earthquake in AD 115. He had been responsible for the construction of a magnificent bath complex and a large hall which could be used for concerts and competitions in music or oratory. Agrippa detailed his munificence in a long inscription listing the various offices he had held on the town council and several other benefactions: 'he also founded the baths and the portico in front of them which adjoins the main street and the adjacent hall and donated all of the land which he purchased from his own funds'. Agrippa went on carefully to catalogue the bronze sculptures he had commissioned for the baths: one group of Theseus and the Minotaur, and another of Apollo and Marsyas, a satyr who rashly challenged the god to a musical contest and, once defeated, was flayed alive. This second group may also have been Agrippa's gently witty commentary on the ambitions of those aspiring performers who competed for prizes in the adjacent hall.

Agrippa's bronzes are a reminder that civic generosity and its display were not confined to building. He himself had sponsored distributions of grain and expensive olive oil to his fellow-citizens. In Ephesus (as described in Chapter 2), Caius Vibius Salutaris funded a magnificent parade in honour of Artemis and the emperor Trajan. Other benefactors aimed to advertise their home towns' cultural credentials. In the mid-120s Caius Julius Demosthenes, a wealthy citizen in the undistinguished city of Oenoanda in south-western Turkey, proposed to endow a four-yearly cultural festival which was to run for three weeks and include competitions in poetry, comic and tragic acting, singing accompanied by the lyre, and oratory. The inscription which records Demosthenes' benefaction and the arrangements for the Demostheneia, as the festival was to be known, is punctilious in pointing out that these were approved by the emperor Hadrian himself and warmly applauded by the town council.

> The council has commended Demosthenes for his unstinting goodwill towards his home town and for his present love of honour, his unsurpassed magnanimity, and for his devotion to the divinely-favoured emperors and has honoured him with every honour. The council has also decreed that the festival should be adorned in every way and that the devotion towards the emperor who has ratified it should be fulfilled in its entirety.

Extravagant inscriptions were matched by idealized images. The official portraits of municipal worthies that crowded the public spaces of every town were designed to impress onlookers with their solidity and easy air of social superiority. In Cuicul in Algeria, when the town council voted statues to the brothers Cosinii, particularly praising Lucius 'because of his munificence', it was Caius who paid for their erection on either side of the main entrance to the market place. In Apamea in Syria, a series of substantial stone brackets, fixed at head-height along the façade of the new baths, supported marble statues of Lucius Julius Agrippa who had so generously funded the whole complex. These multiple images, which looked down on all passers-by, were dedicated by those grateful for the influential assistance of a grandee whom they were pleased to praise publicly as 'founder, patron, and benefactor'.

In towns throughout the empire, the grandiloquent claims of leading citizens to admiring accolades were permanently chiselled in stone. What at first could strike us as a kind of smug self-satisfaction might better be thought of as a more pressing need by leading families to advertise their superior standing. This was a brittle society in which status had continually to be reaffirmed. Lasting memorials to near-bankrupting gestures of generosity set a marker against which rivals or newcomers were forced to compete.

Successes were to be celebrated in both public and private. A splendid mid 3rd-century mosaic from a substantial country house at Smirat in modern Tunisia challenged those who saw it to think about their position in the world. Magnificently attired, Magerius, the owner of the house, is shown presiding over a wild-beast hunt, a moment of munificence in the amphitheatre here captured for all his visitors to see, on prominent display like a modern photograph of a meeting with royalty or the president. Four fighters, Mamertinus, Spittara, Bullarius, and Hilarinus, triumph over four leopards, Crispinus, Romanus, Luxurius, and Victor (but clearly not in this case). In the centre a young servant holds a large silver tray with four bulging money-bags. A long text worked into the mosaic records the acclamations of the crowd. These were proofs that such liberality was recognized by Magerius' fellow-citizens as justifying both wealth and position. No doubt too they impressed his inferiors and caused his equals to pause to calibrate their own and their families' claims to public honour. Certainly, all would have appreciated the force of the rhythmic shouts of an approving crowd repeatedly chanting the name of their benefactor: MAGERII, MAGERII, 'Magerius! Magerius!' In Magerius' grand country

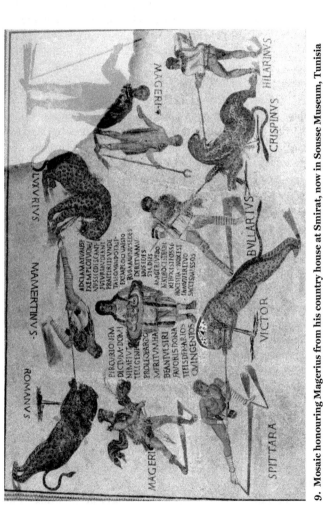

9. Mosaic honouring Magerius from his country house at Smirat, now in Sousse Museum, Tunisia

house, the large mosaic commemorating his achievements carefully preserved that precious moment of public praise for privileged private viewing. It was an attempt to make an instant of unchallenged social superiority last a lifetime. HOC EST HABERE, HOC EST POSSE, 'This is what it is to possess! This is what it is to be powerful!'

The limits of loyalty

Whether local elites were motivated principally by a deep-felt loyalty to the Roman empire or by the pragmatic promotion of their own position within an imperial system it is difficult to say. In an empire established by bloody conquest, where open dissent or revolt brought a rapid and uncompromising response, it is problematic to talk of 'winning hearts and minds' or of 'loyalty' or 'enthusiasm' without these quickly and inevitably shading into more cynical or short-term calculations of advantage. A similar hesitation must also mark any too sweeping claim of the benefits of Roman 'civilization'. In his biography of Cnaeus Julius Agricola, posted to Britain as governor in AD 77, the historian Cornelius Tacitus offered a barbed commentary on the promotion of empire. In this far-flung province Agricola aimed to advance urbanization, to build Roman-style houses and temples, to educate the sons of local worthies in the classics, and to encourage the wearing of togas rather than barbarian trousers. 'As for the Britons', remarked Tacitus, 'who had no experience of any of this, they called it civilization, although in reality it was part of their enslavement.'

On the whole, most provincials would have resisted such a stark analysis. Their experience of empire was often much more complex than a clear-cut choice between opportunistic complicity in the enforcement of Roman rule or inevitable oppression by a conquering power. In the early 3rd century AD, a wealthy resident of Hadrumetum (modern Sousse on the coast of Tunisia) commissioned a series of fine mosaics for his house. One shows the poet Virgil seated with an open scroll in his hand. Clearly legible are

10. Mosaic of Virgil and the Muses from a house in Hadrumetum (modern Sousse in Tunisia), now in Bardo Museum, Tunis

the opening lines of the *Aeneid*. Behind Virgil stand Melpomene and Calliope, the Muses of tragedy and epic. Calliope reads from a scroll, Melpomene, holding a tragic mask, listens intently. The poet, reflective and austere, sits with his feet resting on a stool.

How are we to understand this mosaic of Rome's greatest poet? It might be taken as evidence of the wholesale absorption by African elites of one of the key elements of Roman imperial ideology. But there are other possibilities. Far away from metropolitan Rome in North Africa – the North Africa of a defeated Carthage – the story of Aeneas might have been thought about differently. Here not all might have applauded Aeneas' abandonment of Dido or accepted his divine mission as sufficient justification for his actions. We should not simply assume that the commissioner of the Virgil mosaic in Hadrumetum was an unquestioning supporter of Roman imperial ideology and its claims 'to pacify, to impose the rule of law, to spare the conquered, battle down the proud'. Perhaps, when he recited the *Aeneid* to his friends after dinner, we might imagine that this wealthy African's sympathies lay more with the defeated Carthaginian Dido than the victorious Roman Aeneas.

For the locally powerful in the Mediterranean world, the process of adopting distinctively Roman habits was not so much a demonstration of supine acquiescence as a process of unavoidable – and often profitable – accommodation with a ruling power. It was an accommodation that might also admit of the maintenance of local traditions and sensibilities without these inevitably being seen as indications of resistance. No doubt the commissioner of the Virgil mosaic was a generous supporter of the public building schemes that lent a certain grandeur to Hadrumetum's forum. Like Dio Chrysostom in Bithynia-Pontus, he had perhaps held high office on the town council. He certainly wished to present himself to his peers as well versed in the Latin classics.

Nor should that enthusiasm for the common culture of empire be seen as in some way diminished or faked if it also stood alongside a recognition that much of North Africa had once been under Carthaginian rule. After all, the government of the Roman empire depended on a welding together of local and imperial interests to the mutual advantage of rulers and ruled. That said, Tacitus' jibe about the short distance between civilization and enslavement had a sharp point. For all its evident benefits, it might reasonably be doubted whether the establishment of a unified imperial culture would have been so swift or so successful if it had not been backed by force, or if its possession and advertisement had not been seen as an effective means of dealing with that hard fact.

Though rarely deployed, the threat of Roman retaliation for

perceived provincial resistance hung like a storm cloud over the towns of empire. No matter how skilfully elites maintained their own influence in their localities, their privileged position rested precisely on a continued willingness to act as mediators of Roman rule. In the face of reprisals, local status or even Roman citizenship counted for little. In the 60s AD, while governor in Spain, the future emperor Galba ordered a convicted poisoner to be crucified along with other criminals. When the condemned man appealed against the sentence on the grounds that he was a Roman citizen, Galba instructed that – in public recognition of his superior status – his cross should be set up higher than the rest and painted white.

'You need to imitate an actor', the Greek philosopher and essayist Plutarch (a contemporary of Dio Chrysostom) counselled a friend and aspiring local politician. Avoid too great a confidence in the security of your own position. Stick closely to your script, 'and do not go beyond the degree of freedom in rhythm and metre permitted by those in authority'. On taking up municipal office, Plutarch advised, it is sensible to recall the words which the great 5th-century BC Athenian statesman Pericles regularly repeated to himself: 'Be careful, Pericles, you are ruling free men, you are ruling Greeks, Athenian citizens.' In addition, you should say to yourself: 'You who rule are also ruled, you rule a city subject to governors, the agents of the emperor.' Mutual advantage had its limits. When push came to coercive shove, local elites – for all their much-prized autonomy and hard-won possession of Roman citizenship – were inescapably part of an empire. Successful civic leaders might well have agreed with Plutarch's shrewd assessment: 'do not have too great a pride or confidence' in your position; always bear in mind that you conduct your affairs and those of your city with 'the boots of the Roman governor just above your head'.

Chapter 4
History wars

Foundation and empire

In the 130s AD, the Roman emperor Hadrian invaded Athens. This was warfare without bloodshed: the emperor's attack on the cultural capital of the eastern Mediterranean relied not on crack legionary troops or superior military logistics, but rather on armies of construction workers and careful town planning. Hadrian had long paraded his love of Greek culture. He was the first emperor to travel extensively through the provinces of empire, and as a tourist and not a campaigning general; he was the first emperor to take a sustained and active intellectual interest in the ancient history and monuments of the eastern Mediterranean world.

In Athens, Hadrian's new Library dwarfed the buildings of the ancient Agora, dominating the city's civic centre where six centuries earlier (when Rome had struggled to control even central Italy) citizens had gathered to transact the judicial and administrative business of a democratic state. The Library enclosed a quadrangle surrounded by a vast hundred-column portico of luxurious violet-veined Phrygian marble from quarries in Asia Minor; the interior with its shining gilt ceilings was sumptuously decorated with rare paintings and statues, and expensively embellished with translucent alabaster. This was imperial architecture at its most extravagant. Unashamedly glorying in its baroque brilliance,

Hadrian's Library was an unmistakable proclamation of Roman wealth and power at the centre of the most famous city in the Greek world.

In Athens, Hadrian also finished one of the largest temples ever constructed in the Roman empire. The great shrine to Olympian Zeus – the Olympieion – had been started in the 6th century BC (before Athens was a fully-fledged democracy). Building work had been sporadic and costly; the most recent patron, a century before Hadrian, was the emperor Augustus. Hadrian celebrated the temple's completion in person during a visit to Athens in 131–132, dedicating a colossal chryselephantine (ivory and gold) statue of Zeus. Although the complex is now in ruins and the giant statue disappeared long ago, the point of such gargantuan magnificence is still obvious to the modern visitor. Clearly visible on the top of the Acropolis which rises behind the Olympieion is the Parthenon. This exquisite temple to Athena was completed in the 430s BC under Pericles, democratic Athens' greatest statesman. High above the city, the Parthenon stood as an enduring symbol of Athenian independence and a reminder of one of the most remarkable political experiments in Antiquity.

Hadrian's imperial challenge to Athens' past was more than architectural. The dedication of the Olympieion also marked the inauguration of a new organization of Greek cities, the Panhellenion (literally 'All-Greek'). The Panhellenion covered five Roman provinces, extending far beyond mainland Greece to include cities in Macedonia, Thrace, Asia Minor, Crete, Rhodes, and North Africa. It was presided over by a senior executive officer (*archon*) and a council of delegates (*Panhellenes*) elected by member-states from amongst their most prominent citizens. Hadrian envisaged a permanent international federation, embracing not only ancient foundations such as Athens, Sparta, Corinth, and Argos, but also including those cities across the eastern Mediterranean which could demonstrate a close connection with 'old Greece'.

11. Olympieion in Athens, with the Acropolis and Parthenon behind

Some claims to Hellenic status had echoes in the mythical past. In an official communiqué issued three years after the foundation of the Panhellenion, Hadrian himself intervened in a dispute between the cities of Cyrene (on the fertile heights above the coastal plain in Libya) and Ptolemais-Barca (about 90 kilometres to the west). Cyrene's Hellenic credentials were not in doubt. It had been founded in the late 7th century BC by Greek colonists from Thera (modern Santorini). Hadrian also confirmed that Ptolemais-Barca should be admitted to the Panhellenion; its citizens, in the emperor's resonant phrase, were 'true-born Greeks', but the city was instructed to send only one delegate to the council whereas Cyrene was permitted to send two. Hadrian's ruling perhaps reflected ancient history: in the mid 6th century BC, Ptolemais-Barca had not been established directly by Greeks, but by colonists from Cyrene. The emperor's ratification of Cyrene's superior Greekness was inscribed and proudly displayed. No further proof of the authenticity of the city's claims was required.

Other cities sought to secure their place in this privileged Hellenic past. Cibyra in south-western Turkey had been cited by the early 1st-century geographer Strabo as a non-Greek foundation. Over a century later, in a successful bid to join the Panhellenion, the city had fabricated a completely different account of its origins connecting it closely with both Sparta and Athens. This was a persuasive fiction. Existing members of the Panhellenion were eager to collude with Cibyra's inflated re-invention of its own identity as:

> a colony of the Spartans and related to the Athenians, friendly to Rome and in the commonwealth of Greece [that is, the Panhellenion] amongst the most highly reputed and greatest cities in the province of Asia because of its Greek ancestry and its ancient friendship and goodwill towards the Romans, and because it has been honoured with great privileges by the god Hadrian.

Hadrian's Panhellenion re-shaped the Greek world. It brought together in a single institutional framework many cities that had never before been connected and indeed in the past had often been bitter enemies. Athens was designated the Panhellenion's headquarters. Here Hadrian established a four-yearly religious festival, the Panhellenia, first held in 137. In addition, he inaugurated the Hadrianeia (a festival associated with emperor-worship) and the Olympieia (associated with Olympian Zeus). These three festivals were each designated a 'sacred contest'; winners in the various athletic and cultural competitions were assured significant privileges in their home cities, including a procession to mark their victorious return, substantial tax breaks, and free meals at public expense. Hadrian also conferred the same status on the Panathenaea. This ancient festival in honour of Athena was said to have been instituted by Theseus, the city's legendary founder. Theseus had ruled Athens after his return from Crete, where he had secured lasting fame by escaping from the labyrinth and slaying the Minotaur.

The concentration of four sacred festivals in one city, without precedent in the entire history of Greece, underlined the central importance of Athens in this reorganized and improved Hellenic past. The extensive re-modelling of the city – now more Greek than any other – was celebrated in the recently completed temple to Olympian Zeus. The entrance was flanked by four statues of Hadrian, two in marble and two in porphyry (a hard, deep-purple Egyptian stone that since pharaonic times had been associated with rulership). Behind the temple towered a colossal statue of the emperor erected in his honour by the Athenians. The precinct itself was filled with bronze statues of Hadrian Olympios dedicated by cities from all over the Greek world. The message was clear. In almost identical inscriptions from nearly 100 altars found in excavations in Athens, Hadrian was routinely praised as 'Saviour, Founder, and Olympios'. Ringed with repeated images of the emperor, it was Hadrian's Olympieion – and not Pericles' Parthenon – that now claimed the symbolic and religious heart of the city.

Other Greek cities reiterated the insistent themes of Hadrian's Hellenic renaissance. Twenty-one in the eastern Mediterranean are known to have celebrated festivals with the title Hadrianeia; 15 added the epithet 'Hadriane' to their names; 9 more called themselves Hadrianopolis, 'the city of Hadrian'. In Hadrian's empire, local and imperial enthusiasms combined to create a unity and cultural cohesion never before enjoyed by the Greek world. In the 2nd century AD, a new corporate commitment to a common heritage amongst 'Greek' cities helped suppress the memory of ancient conflicts. The defeat of Athens and her allies by Sparta at the end of the Peloponnesian War 600 years before was to be erased; so too the city's subjugation in the 4th century BC by Philip of Macedon, the father of Alexander the Great. A fractured past was to be forgotten. Hadrian's benefactions ensured that Athens was now the unchallenged capital of a brave new Panhellenic world which stretched from Asia Minor to North Africa. A Roman emperor could at last succeed where Greek history had so obviously failed.

Dreaming of Greece

Perhaps unsurprisingly, not all welcomed these radical Roman revisions of Greece's past. In the late 170s, a generation after Hadrian's death, Pausanias, a native of Lydia in western Turkey, finally completed his *Description of Greece*, the culmination of nearly 20 years of extensive travel and research. In his *Description*, Pausanias set out to lead his readers on a tour of 'all things Greek'; a series of meticulously plotted itineraries started in Athens and then moved out across the Peloponnese and the southern mainland. Pausanias' especial interest was in sacred places, their history, and their monuments. For the most part, his records of the several hundred sites which he visited are detailed and accurate; their authority has been repeatedly confirmed by modern excavations. It was Pausanias' account of the Lion Gate at Mycenae and his observation that the tombs of Agamemnon and other Homeric heroes were located 'inside the walls' that inspired Heinrich Schliemann to excavate the upper city in 1876. The result was one of the most spectacular archaeological finds ever made in Greece. What matters is not whether the beautiful gold funerary masks and valuable grave goods which Schliemann found actually belonged to the victors of the Trojan War, but that Pausanias reliably reported a tradition of ancient burial already 1,700 years old when he visited the ruins of Mycenae.

Like any good guide, Pausanias does not offer an exhaustive catalogue of everything that can be seen. Rather, he presents a very particular view of the territory through which he travels. His *Description* provides a systematic survey of 'the things most worthy of mention'; 'a selection of the most noteworthy objects' which ought to be of interest to those seeking to understand Greece under Roman rule. In Athens, Pausanias notes the building programme of Hadrian, whom he praises as 'contributing greatly to the well-being of his various subjects', but his attention is firmly focused on Antiquity. In the Agora, he lingers over those monuments that mark the foundation of the city, celebrate the heroic deeds of Theseus, or commemorate the central role of the Athenians in resisting the Persian invasions of the 5th century BC. There is scant reference to any building undertaken since the Roman conquest of Greece, and only a comparatively cursory mention of Hadrian's new Library.

Pausanias gives a longer description of the Olympieion, although less than a third is devoted to its recent completion by Hadrian. Here there is no time to stare in admiration at the achievements of a Roman emperor, what matters are the reminders of a mythical Greek past. Rather than looking up at the towering columns of the temple or gazing in awe at the crowd of bronze Hadrians that populated its precinct, the visitor is deftly guided to the edge of a muddy depression about 40 centimetres wide. This, in Pausanias' view, is what anyone interested 'in all things Greek' should see. It links both tourist and reader to the very beginnings of Greece. It is a memorial of the great flood which once upon a time engulfed the world, and of its survivor Deucalion, whose son Hellen was the ultimate progenitor of the Hellenic race. The depression near the Olympieion is said to be the sump into which the flood waters finally receded. Here is a closer connection with 'old Greece' than the magnificent temple and the statues of a Roman emperor who claimed – as 'Saviour and Founder' – to have established the Panhellenic world anew.

Pausanias' tour of Athens puts Hadrian in his proper place. It measures his restoration of Greek culture against the surviving traces which reveal the overwhelming superiority of the original. Moving now from the Agora up to the Acropolis, Pausanias notes, merely in passing, that a statue of Hadrian had been placed in the Parthenon. Certainly, this deserves no more than a glance next to the much longer treatment of the enormous 5th-century chryselephantine statue of Athena which still dominated the temple's interior. 'The statue of Athena is standing . . . she holds an image of victory four cubits [about 2 metres] high and in the other hand a spear. A shield is placed at her feet and just next to the spear is a serpent.' Nor is this contemplation of the classical

12. Remains of the Temple to Rome and Augustus on the Acropolis in Athens, in front of the east end of the Parthenon

past to be interrupted. For nearly two centuries before Pausanias visited the Acropolis, a circular temple nearly 10 metres high, dedicated to Rome and the emperor Augustus, had stood directly in front of the Parthenon, blocking a clear view of its eastern façade. In Pausanias' *Description*, no mention at all is made of this building. In this guide to 'all things Greek' these obvious Roman blots on an ancient landscape were simply to be effaced.

Outside Athens, Pausanias' deliberate failure to describe recent intrusions into a pristine Hellenic world is even more clearly marked. Few of the monuments he points out are later than the 3rd century BC. At Corinth, most of the city is passed over in silence; it had been razed by a victorious Roman army in 146 BC and refounded a century later by Julius Caesar. What matters instead are the ancient stories of Corinthian kings, gods, and heroes. Here

Bellerophon is commemorated by an antique shrine dedicated to Athena, 'the Breaker-in', the first to bridle Pegasus, his mighty winged horse. In visiting Patrae (modern Patras on the southern shore of the Gulf of Corinth), Pausanias noted that the city had been substantially enlarged by the emperor Augustus, who had systematically destroyed surrounding settlements and transplanted their populations. The disruptive consequences were still painfully evident to the discerning observer. Fifteen kilometres inland at Pherae (once an autonomous town, but now subject to Patrae), a sacred grove had been despoiled: 'here there is neither temple nor images; the locals told me that the images had been carried off to Rome'.

This was stark evidence of subjugation; evidence which it was best to pass quickly by on a journey through a greener and more pleasant pre-conquest land. For his fellow-travellers, Pausanias offered the comfortable experience of a tour through an imaginary Greece. And like Hadrian's Panhellenion, Pausanias' Greece was more Hellenic than the original. His was a nostalgic yearning for something that never was; a vision of the past as it should have been: a unified Greece with Athens at its centre. (Those city-states allied to Sparta who had caused Athens' defeat at the end of the 5th century BC were to be dismissed as nothing better than 'murderers and practically the wreckers of Greece'.) Above all, Pausanias' *Description* presented a coherent network of ancient places whose identity could best be revealed to a curious traveller by a knowledgeable guide who could search out 'all things Greek'. And unlike Hadrian's Panhellenion, the integrity and wholeness of this idealized Greece was not circumscribed by Roman imperial command; rather, it was deep-rooted in an aboriginal sense of its own origins, religion, and mythology.

Parallel pasts

If Pausanias sought to expunge the all too visible impact of foreign conquest on an enchanted classical landscape, the historian and philosopher Plutarch – also responding to the intrusion of a new imperial power in an old world – sought rather to coordinate and compare the habits and histories of both the Greeks and the Romans. In the first two decades of the 2nd century (across the reigns of Trajan and Hadrian), Plutarch completed 46 biographies of famous Greeks and Romans. These were arranged in pairs; so, for example, Alexander the Great partnered Julius Caesar; the outstanding Athenian politician Pericles joined Fabius Maximus Cunctator, 'the Delayer', who in the Second Punic War had forced Hannibal to withdraw from Italy; and Theseus (the founder of Athens) was coupled with Romulus (the founder of Rome).

The principal purpose of these *Parallel Lives* was to offer a series of historical scenarios which would encourage readers to consider the ethical issues involved. Plutarch concentrated on the lives of statesmen and generals, firmly believing that their characters were most clearly revealed in their actions. Taken together the paired biographies invited the reader to think through particular problems: how to control passions (anger, desire, and ambition); how to judge the effects of up-bringing and education; how to display humanity, forbearance, and compassion. Both Greeks and Romans provided positive and negative examples. Pericles and Fabius offered models of wise statesmen who faced with the perils of war stand calm against a protesting mob. Alexander the Great and Julius Caesar invited debate on the benefits and dangers of ambition. Their parallel lives exposed how a desire for power and glory can inspire great deeds, but also provoke disaster.

Plutarch's concern to present a range of ethical debates for the edification of his readers is of primary importance in the selection and arrangement of his material. It is most clearly on display in the formal comparisons that concluded each pair of biographies. In his

Life of Romulus, Plutarch doubted one ancient criticism of the founder of Rome: that in a heated dispute over the site of the new city he had killed his twin brother, Remus. But Romulus' 'unreasonable anger, his hasty and ill-advised wrath' could not be ignored. In Plutarch's view, it was Romulus' unbridled behaviour that had encouraged one of his companions to slay Remus on the spot. The parallel was with a famous Greek family feud that had its origin in the accusations of Theseus' wife, Phaedra, against her stepson, Hippolytus, whom she alleged had made passionate advances to her. Trusting his wife, Theseus abused and cursed his son, refusing to countenance his claims of innocence. (In truth, it was Hippolytus who had been solicited by Phaedra, who, when rejected, sought her revenge.) In Plutarch's view, Theseus, although equally guilty of 'unreasonable anger', was nevertheless 'foiled by love, envy, and a woman's calumnies, whose overwhelming force few men have escaped'. Most importantly (at least in the version of the story Plutarch chose to tell), Theseus' uncontrolled passion had led only to unjust words, while Romulus' had inspired his friend to murder. 'For these reasons then,' Plutarch concluded, 'one would vote in favour of Theseus', preferring the founder of Athens to the founder of Rome.

In making such difficult judgement-calls, Plutarch adhered closely to conventional Greek ethical ideas. One key text was Plato's *Republic*, the great Athenian philosopher's blueprint for an ideal society. One of Plato's central concerns was self-restraint. In men of action, he argued, some degree of anger was necessary to inspire bravery in warfare; but in a virtuous man, anger must always be tempered with calmness. In the end, Theseus – though still some distance from realizing this ideal – was better able to curb the consequences of his rage than Romulus. Control of the passions was one of the chief objects of education. In praising Numa, Romulus' successor and the second of the seven legendary kings of early Rome, Plutarch had no doubt that his ability to frame just laws was rooted in strict self-discipline: 'his cultivation was a result of education, enduring hardship, and philosophy . . . reckoning true manliness to consist in the confinement of one's passions within one's self through the use of reason'.

This then is the core of Plutarch's enterprise: to offer a series of double portraits of Greeks and Romans and to judge them both by explicitly Greek ethical norms. On one level, the *Parallel Lives* assert the comparability of Greek and Roman political and military figures. Matching one against another, conquerors and conquered are presented on an equal footing. That too was an exercise best and most effectively undertaken by the writing of history. (The latest *Lives* are of Julius Caesar and Mark Antony. To go further would mean confronting Augustus, and with what Greek might he be credibly paired?) Most importantly, Plutarch suggests that both Greeks and Romans can be evaluated by a single set of criteria which are unashamedly and unmistakably Greek. It is perhaps unsurprising that in 20 (out of 23) of these paired biographies, the opening life is Greek. In these *Parallel Lives* it is the Greek that sets the terms of inquiry for the Roman; it is Greek morality and philosophy by which the strengths and failings of individuals are to be assessed. Taken together, these biographies make a radical and arresting claim: that Roman history is to be understood most perfectly from a Greek perspective. The resulting paradox is delightful: in Plutarch's view, outstanding Romans are in fact inspiring examples of traditional Greek virtues in action.

The empire writes back

Of course, it would be too simple to think of Plutarch or Pausanias as active opponents of Roman power. They would not have supported Boudica and her British revolt nor have committed suicide with the last of the Jewish freedom-fighters at Masada. Their works incited no riots; they did not inspire armed rebellion; no emperors were moved to suppress them. Indeed, Plutarch (like many of the Mediterranean's landowning elite) was a beneficiary of empire. He inherited estates in Boeotia in central Greece; he held high municipal office in his local town of Chaeronea; he enjoyed the privileges of Roman citizenship and the friendship of a number of wealthy and powerful Romans. Rather than as open encouragements to resist Roman rule, what makes both Plutarch's and Pausanias' works interesting is a clear recognition that the imposition of empire not only involves substantial political, economic, and social rupture in the present, but also has an inseparable and significant impact on the past. Indeed, in addition to effective administration, tax collection, and the maintenance of law and order, part of what marks out a ruling power (long after the bloodshed of conquest and the parade of peace and prosperity restored) is its ability selectively to refashion for its own ends the history of its subject peoples.

In the early 2nd century AD, Hadrian provoked a historical revolution. Those pasts incompatible with the comfortable image of a munificent emperor and a complicit civic elite were effaced. Hadrian's building programme in Jerusalem defiantly ignored the city's Jewish heritage. In 130, while on tour in Judaea, he founded a veteran colony on the site, henceforth to be known as Colonia Aelia Capitolina (Aelius was the emperor's family name). This decision to obliterate Jerusalem is sometimes suggested as one of the factors that may have led to the Jewish revolt of 132–135. Little is known of this insurrection; for a while the rebels, led by the charismatic Shim'on ben Kosiba (or Bar Kochba), waged a successful guerrilla war and minted their own coins proclaiming their intention to rebuild the Temple. But it was not to last. A large Roman force commanded by Hadrian himself crushed the revolt. Reprisals were ruthless: in one account, 50 towns and 985 villages were destroyed and over half a million insurgents slain.

After the Roman victory, building in Jerusalem continued. The forum (in the area of the much later Church of the Holy Sepulchre) was dominated by a temple to Jupiter. For the previous 60 years, since the sack of the city by Roman legions in AD 70 (the victory celebrated on the Arch of Titus in Rome), the Temple Mount had been abandoned. Now it was topped by two statues: one of Jupiter and one of Hadrian on horseback. Strikingly, Jews were strictly forbidden to settle in the city or its territory. Jerusalem, refounded and renamed, was closed to those for whom it was most holy. They were to be treated as permanent outsiders. Aelia Capitolina, extensively re-modelled with a new set of imposing monuments, was fully part of Hadrian's Roman empire; its rebel history – like the Jews themselves – completely purged.

Hadrian's attitude to the Hellenic past was much less brutal. That said, it would clearly be too crude to think of him as a passionate or undiscriminating promoter of all things Greek. His spectacular benefactions to Athens (and to over 200 other cities around the Mediterranean) and his liking for Greek history and literature are more than just expressions of a deeply felt phil-Hellenism. In the cities of empire the building programmes Hadrian sponsored systematically monumentalized a very particular version of the past. In turn, through an explicit association with the emperor himself, that past was incorporated within a very Roman imperial present. On a grand scale, and nowhere more expansively than at the Olympieion in Athens, the emperor was paired with traditional deities whose worship he could legitimately claim to have re-invigorated. At Smyrna, modern Izmir on the Aegean coast of Turkey, the building of a huge temple associated Hadrian closely with Zeus Akraios (Zeus 'dwelling on High'). At Cyzicus, on the southern shore of the Sea of Marmara, Hadrian's own image looked down from the pediment of another gigantic temple to Zeus. At Palmyra, in eastern Syria, the emperor was linked with the ancient gods Ba'alshamin and Dourahloun, now worshipped in an imposing new shrine.

These projects were also the result of civic enthusiasm and private wealth. They allowed local grandees to associate themselves with the emperor and to proclaim their importance on an international scale. In Smyrna, an inscription praising the beautification of the city listed contributions from 25 leading citizens alongside that of Hadrian himself. Such paradoxes are unavoidable: they neatly

capture the everyday consequences of conquest. They are part of
what it is to be subject to an empire. In early 2nd-century Ephesus
the fortnightly procession of silver statues funded by Caius Vibius
Salutaris joined Roman emperors to a local history of heroes,
founding-fathers, and gods. As explored in Chapters 2 and 3, that
close connection between empire and city was crucially important;
but it also involved a celebration of the supremacy of Rome. At
Aphrodisias, the striking display of images of naked emperors
allowed Roman power to be presented according to long-standing
Greek conventions; but it also placed the empire's rulers on the
same level as the Olympian gods. Membership of Hadrian's
Panhellenion required proof of an antique Hellenic ancestry
(something that might be thought attractive to both Plutarch and
Pausanias); but it also entailed collusion with a Roman emperor's
re-creation of the Greek world as it ought to have been.

It is against this seemingly pacific Roman invasion that Plutarch
and Pausanias react. In response, they offer a different version of
the Greek past, and one no less deliberately refashioned. Inevitably
too, their counter-claims are compromised. Pausanias' Greece (the
southern mainland, Attica, and the Peloponnese) is entirely
contained within the Roman province of Achaea. Pausanias'
itinerary follows the contours of a Roman imperial geography
(incomprehensible to any Greek living in the 5th century BC), a
tacit admission that the 'old Greece' which his *Description* seeks
to evoke was not unified until the imposition of Roman rule.
Similarly, the historical project of Plutarch's *Parallel Lives* is
clearly implicated in a recognition that for the biographer or the
philosopher it is the rise of the Roman empire to its secure position
of world dominance which above all demands explanation.

In the 1st and 2nd centuries AD, the coercive effect of Roman power
was inescapable: in both the present and the past. For the most
part, as Plutarch and Pausanias neatly exemplify, the choice was
never a straightforward one between collusion or opposition. (In
the end, it is only those who have never been subject to conquest

who can afford to think in such clear-cut terms.) Even so, the absence of open resistance – with the notable exception of the Jews – should not lull us into thinking that Hadrian's building campaign was without any sharp edge. For Roman emperors, the past was available for appropriation. It could be reconfigured to remove the scars of conquest and to emphasize the close relationship between rulers and ruled. For some Greek intellectuals – no doubt in danger of seeking comfortable refuge in an ivory-tower world – the past was the only place left in which the fantasy of liberation could still be played out, or at least not forgotten: in Pausanias' Greece, free of Roman monuments; in Plutarch's biographies, in which Greek ethics and philosophy offered the best explanation of events and the best models for a virtuous life.

History is an inevitable casualty of empire. In Athens, the city above all others where Hadrian made his mark, an elegant arch was erected near the Olympieion to commemorate the emperor's generosity towards the city. On its western face an inscription proclaimed: 'This is Athens, the former city of Theseus.' For those slow to comprehend, a slogan on the opposite side reiterated the point: 'This is the city of Hadrian, not Theseus.' Like much of Hadrian's other building, the arch and its inscriptions can be embraced as an enthusiastic endorsement of Greek history. In the midst of the city of Pericles and the headquarters of the Panhellenion, a Roman emperor is seen wittily to suggest his own parallel life, here pairing himself with the city's first founder. Or Hadrian's claim to match Theseus' first foundation can be understood as a strident public proclamation of imperial dominance over Athens, past and present.

Of course, both explanations are possible, both readings correct. In the end, it is precisely the uncertainty that matters. Such deliberate ambiguities allowed local elites to cheer on a Roman emperor in ways compatible with long-standing traditions and to appreciate the sophisticated history-writing of Greek-speaking thinkers such as Plutarch or Pausanias. That rulers like Hadrian should forcefully

13. Arch of Hadrian in Athens, with Olympieion behind

assert their superiority on their own monuments was unsurprising.
Equally, it was only to be expected that, in his own carefully
choreographed tour of Athens, Pausanias would remain resolutely
blind to the intrusive presence – at the very centre of the Greek
world – of an arch in honour of a Roman emperor.

Chapter 5
Christians to the lions

Blood on the sand

In summer AD 177 at Lugdunum (modern Lyon in southern France), it was fiesta time, and in the amphitheatre Christians were on the programme. Their fellow-believers later set down their eyewitness accounts of what happened. First, Maturus and Sanctus were brought in. They were subjected to every kind of torture; they ran the gauntlet of whips; they were mauled by wild animals; they endured all that the shouts of the excited crowd demanded. Next, Attalus and Alexander. They too were tortured and finally strapped to a heated iron chair which seared their flesh. On the last day of the festival, the slave woman Blandina was led into the amphitheatre. After the whips, after the lions, after the red-hot plates, she was flung into a net and offered to a bull. 'After being tossed for a while by the animal, she no longer had any sense of what was happening thanks to her hope, the firmness of her beliefs, and her communion with Christ.'

For the inhabitants of 2nd-century Lyon, Christians were part of a good day out; part of the entertainment; part of the show. The crowd – like the lions – roared. But it is also important to emphasize that in this story (and in many other tales of violence and brutality like it) the onlookers who enthusiastically cheered were not a disorderly rabble of local louts and layabouts. This was no hysterical mob; rather, good solid citizenry for whom publicly organized violence was a serious and absorbing pastime. Society's outcasts (bandits, robbers, condemned criminals, runaway slaves) were expected to perish horribly for the enjoyment of decent, law-abiding people. Similarly, professional fighters (gladiators, wild-beast hunters) were expected to perform. Some spectators were experts on their favourites' skills, training, and careers. For others, these battle-scarred bits-of-rough were the stuff of sexual fantasy.

All who went to the games were deeply involved. In Rome, the emperor Claudius is said to have been so fascinated by the death-agonies of the slain that he ordered their faces to be turned toward him. Indeed, according to the imperial biographer Suetonius, Claudius (himself a physical weakling) was such an enthusiast for gladiatorial violence that he would arrive at the amphitheatre before dawn and not leave during the afternoon when most of the wealthier members of the crowd retired home for their siesta.

Going to the games was one of the practices that went with being a Roman. In amphitheatres access to seating was through a complicated series of ill-lit passages, ramps, and steep staircases. Like the best 19th-century opera houses, these ensured that as far as possible those in the best seats had their own exclusive access to the auditorium. Emerging from the darkness the spectator – still blinking – beheld a striking, sunlit microcosm of his own society; each member dressed in festival best; each seated according to carefully calibrated gradations of age, rank, wealth, and occupation. The emperor Augustus had ordered the seating in theatres to reflect the empire's social hierarchy. In provincial cities, members of the town council occupied the best seats; then male citizens, with married men separated from bachelors; professional associations in designated rows; and citizen boys in a separate block.

No doubt in practice these seemingly rigid classifications were

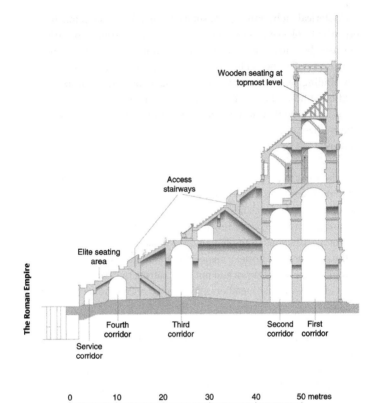

Wooden seating at
topmost level

Access
stairways

Elite seating
area

Fourth
corridor

Third
corridor

Second
corridor

First
corridor

Service
corridor

0   10   20   30   40   50 metres

14. Cross-section of the Colosseum (reconstruction)

blurred (grandees might, for example, invite their friends to sit with
them), but their general intent is clear: the potentially rowdy urban
poor was to be allowed only a very limited presence. In the
Colosseum in Rome, 60% of its 50,000 seats were reserved for well-
off citizens; only 20% at the rear were given over to the urban poor,
non-citizens, and slaves. The remaining space, in cloistered rows
right at the top of the tiered seating (a climb of 220 steps from the
entrance at ground level), was allocated to women. The strict
geometric architecture of an amphitheatre neatly divided the crowd

into clearly recognizable social segments. It mattered where you sat; and where you were seen to be sitting.

In Rome, an emperor at the games presided over a carefully ordered empire in miniature. The acclamations he received from the crowd were an audible register of popular support for the prevailing régime. Seated in the imperial box, the emperor was clearly visible to all. Both Julius Caesar and the late 2nd-century emperor Marcus Aurelius were strongly criticized for catching up on official correspondence instead of enjoying the show. Emperors were expected to pay attention both to the fighting in the arena and to the spectators, who might at any moment demand favours or with shouts of *Habet, hoc habet* – 'He has it! He has got it!' – applaud a winning hit or cheer on the death of a fatally wounded gladiator. Gladiators were trained not only to fight well, but also to die properly, chest out, leaning to the right, head drooping, half-seated on their weapons. This was the dying swan of the Roman world, a cool, formalized way of death, which, if not properly performed, would be loudly booed by a disapproving crowd.

Such carefully staged moments of life and death were part of a set of public extravaganzas whose sheer organization alone demands admiration. For emperors, the financing of these spectaculars proclaimed to all their wealth and position at the apex of society. Before an approving crowd it was in their interests that both blood and money flowed freely. In the funeral games that Julius Caesar staged in honour of his father in 65 BC, the gladiators' armour was made of silver. On other occasions it might be studded with jewels or decorated with peacock or ostrich feathers. In AD 80, the opening of the Colosseum was celebrated by 100 days of games, which included gladiatorial fights and the slaughter of 9,000 wild animals. The spectators were further entertained by the emperor Titus, who threw into the crowd small wooden balls each marked with a sign indicating that they could be exchanged for food or clothing or (for a lucky few) horses, silverware, or slaves.

The striking investment of time, wealth, and emotion that gladiatorial games involved underlines their importance as a display of dominance. The cheers and rhythmic chants of the spectators proclaimed both their communal solidarity and their collective distance from those whom they had come to see butchered. In deciding the fate of a defeated gladiator, the crowd asserted its absolute control over humanity. Fatal games were an interlude of controlled disorder sponsored by society in order to affirm its own security. In that sense, amphitheatres, and the carefully regulated crowds and murderous games they contained, were epitomes of both the violence and the order that helped hold the empire together. In these bloody spectacles violence was presented as an inescapable part of an ordered society, just as war had once been a necessary part of the acquisition of empire.

Importantly too, however successfully violence and order may be compressed into one site, they can never be entirely separated from each other. The stout wooden barricades that cordoned off the arena from the crowd marked out a division which could be crossed, confused, broken down, blurred. In 192, the senator and historian Cassius Dio attended games held by the emperor Commodus, who not only presided, but also fought as a gladiator.

> The games lasted fourteen days. When the emperor was fighting, we senators always attended . . . And there is a thing which the emperor did to us senators which gave us good reason to expect that we were done for. After he had killed an ostrich he cut off its head and came right up to where we were seated, holding the head in his left hand and waving his bloody sword in his right. He said nothing, but grinning he wagged his head, indicating that he would deal with us in the same way. Many who were laughing at him would have been eliminated by the sword there and then (for it was laughter rather than distress which overcame us) if I had not chewed some laurel leaves, which I took from my garland, and persuaded the others who were seated near me to chew theirs, so that by the steady movement of our jaws we might hide the fact that we were laughing.

In Cassius Dio's eyewitness account, the emperor Commodus, maniacally grinning and waving a severed ostrich head, is clearly, and dangerously, on the wrong side of the fence. What Dio later portrayed as amusement at a farcical spectacle, was more likely at the time the nervous, dry laughter of deep fear. To have an emperor waving a severed head at you is not really funny until that emperor himself is safely dead. Dio and his senatorial colleagues must have been panic-stricken. Their terror was well founded. At the games Roman emperors not only emphasized their importance as upholders of social convention, they also underscored their autocratic position by demonstrating their ability to violate society's rules with total immunity.

Emperors were powerful (and were seen to be so); unlike the crowd, seated in their orderly rows, or those slaughtered in the games precisely because they were outsiders, emperors could act however they pleased. They could capriciously cross the boundaries that separated violence and order. An emperor posing as a gladiator was a frightening sight for Cassius Dio and his colleagues precisely because it exposed the weakness of their position as senators and the importance of convention for the maintenance of their status. Unlike emperors, senators had no social room to move. Commodus' potent display of autocratic power challenged everything that Dio stood for, everything he relied upon for the security of his rank and position. It might be possible to laugh later; but, at the time, the only person smiling must have been the emperor: no doubt amused at the sight of rows of bovine senators surreptitiously munching their laurel crowns and hoping that nobody would notice.

What a society does in its leisure time is an important indication of how it seeks to organize its world. Amphitheatres, with the crowds and spectacles they were designed to contain, were places that celebrated both order and violence; places where Roman society and imperial power were on public parade; places where in the middle of its cities members of a militaristic society continued to wage war – sometimes against each other – even in times of peace.

Like the great mediaeval cathedrals of northern Europe, amphitheatres dominated the cityscape of many Roman towns. Alongside armies, taxes, laws, and administration, they helped impose a definitive and recognizable order on the conquered provinces of empire. Fenced off within the confines of an amphitheatre, the brutal process of conquest could be effortlessly re-enacted and (this time) loudly applauded. Bloody spectacles allowed regimented crowds all over the empire to go on campaign without leaving the comfort of their own home towns. And, importantly, in their amphitheatres the spectators always won.

The martyrs' brigade

It was in this same threatening space where Roman society sought to hold in play life and death, violence and order, society and its enemies that many Christians went willingly to their deaths. Martyrdom was not a Christian innovation, it had clear Jewish antecedents; but Christian martyrdom was distinctive in being deliberately sought in front of an unbelieving and hostile crowd. It ran its grim course in one of the most important public places in any Roman city. It intersected directly with the complex compression of violence and order that marked out the Roman experience of games in the amphitheatre.

That martyrdoms were bloody spectaculars should not be doubted. In AD 177, the crowd in Lyon that cheered a group of Christians to their deaths saw one torn on the rack, another fried in an iron chair, a third tossed by a bull, the rest thrown to half-starved lions who ripped their victims limb from limb. Throwing Christians to the lions in the full, public gaze of a well-dressed crowd sitting in orderly rows in an amphitheatre must have seemed a dramatic assertion of Roman majority power over a minority sect. But it is also necessary to maintain some proper sense of proportion. Amidst shows which brought together wild beasts and miscreants from all over the Mediterranean and slaughtered them for the enjoyment of spectators, a few Christians thrown to the lions cannot have caused that much excitement. They were just another group of undesirables to be paraded round, jeered at, and killed.

But for Christians, a martyr's torture and death was not a demoralizing defeat at the hands of a hostile and unforgiving community. Martyrdom was a triumph; it was a dramatic public act of defiance in the very place where Roman society had chosen to put itself on display and to demonstrate its own superiority. For Christians in the cities of the empire, martyrdom became a signal affirmation of their faith and a potent demonstration of their open contempt for Roman order. A public profession of Christianity and a horrifically memorable public execution were central to martyrdom's claim to be a successful act of protest and a rallying point for believers. No other death sanctified an otherwise seemingly irrational desire for self-sacrifice.

Christians – like capricious emperors – deliberately set out to challenge the carefully constructed balance of order and violence at the centre of gladiatorial games. Emperors thereby demonstrated that they stood powerfully above the concerns and conventions of this world; Christians thereby proclaimed that they were only concerned with the world to come. In the early 2nd century, Ignatius, bishop of Antioch in Syria, declared uncompromisingly on his way to martyrdom:

> From Syria all the way to Rome I am fighting with wild beasts by land and sea, by night and day . . . Let there come upon me fire and the cross, and packs of wild beasts, laceration, dismemberment, the dislocation of bones, the severing of limbs, the crushing of the whole body . . . For I am the wheat of God and I am ground by the teeth of wild beasts so that I may be found to be the pure bread of Christ.

Above all, it was martyrdom's power to subvert that mattered. The bloody stories of martyrs' sufferings were read out in church. These vivid and detailed accounts of Christian deaths allowed their victories to be repeated at every reading. When in the mid-150s Polycarp, bishop of Smyrna (modern Izmir), was burned at the stake, according to the account of those Christians who claimed to have witnessed the event:

> The flames formed into the shape of a vault, just like a ship's sail bellying out in the wind, and encircled the martyr's body like a wall. He was in their midst not as burning flesh but rather as bread being baked, or like gold and silver being refined in a furnace. From it we perceived such a sweet smelling fragrance as though it were smoking incense or some other costly perfume.

Christian martyrdom turned the Roman world upside-down. In Christian eyes, the mutilated bodies of the martyrs were beautiful to behold. To the Christian nose, the smell of singed flesh was overpowering in its scented sweetness. Beautification was a necessary prelude to beatification. And, importantly, in their martyr acts the Christians always won.

Roman reactions

By and large, Romans regarded Christians as a laughable and easily expendable group. At the turn of the 2nd century AD, 25 years after the 'Martyrs of Lyon' went to their deaths, a graffito was scratched on the wall plaster of a building that formed part of the imperial palace on the Palatine Hill in the centre of Rome. It shows the crucifixion of a man with the head of a donkey; beside the cross an onlooker raises his arms in an attitude of prayer; underneath an awkwardly executed inscription reads (in Greek), 'Alexander worships his God.' This is clearly neither a sophisticated nor penetrating critique of Christian religion. But the point (in all its crassness) is clear: Christians are a joke; Alexander is a fool; he worships his god – a crucified donkey.

In similar vein, Minucius Felix, a lawyer and Christian convert

15. Anti-Christian graffito from the Paedagogium, part of the imperial palace on the Palatine Hill, Rome

writing in the early 3rd century, filled out his imaginary dialogue between a Christian and a pagan by including some of the abuse to which he claimed Christians were regularly subjected.

> They recognise each other by secret signs and marks. . . . I hear that they consecrate and, following some absurdly ignorant belief,

worship the head of a donkey, the lowest of all beasts. . . . The stories of the initiation of newcomers are as revolting as they are well known. An infant covered with dough to deceive the unsuspecting is placed next to the person to be inducted into the sacred rites. The novice is incited to inflict what seem to be harmless blows on the surface of the dough and by these unseen and secret wounds the infant is killed. The blood – and this an unholy outrage – they lap up greedily; the limbs they eagerly tear apart.

These insults should not be taken too seriously, either as a description of early Christianity or of what ordinary Romans really believed about it. (Although, one should perhaps not be too surprised at the accusations of cannibalism. A religion whose central rite involves the symbolic consumption of the body and blood of its founder might perhaps expect such an attack.) In this passage factual accuracy is unimportant; what matters above all is that it is pure abuse. Here abuse, as it so often does, marks out boundaries and reinforces group solidarity. That is the lesson of every junior school playground. Listening to abuse, we often learn more about those making the insults than about their targets. For some Romans, accusing Christians of bizarre, inhuman, or anti-social practices was also a way of defining what was acceptable in their own society. Colourful accusations against Christians helped establish what was properly Roman.

For many, what was most puzzling was Christian martyrs' steadfast refusal to participate in Roman society, to enjoy the benefits of empire, to show due and proper deference to the emperor. No doubt too, the martyrs' religiously inspired death frenzies were difficult to comprehend. As a way of publicly expressing belief, in contrast to the carefully regulated parades and festivals central to well-ordered civic society, martyrdom must have seemed both mystifying and unappealing. Even so, on the whole, the Roman authorities were not keen to become involved in seeking out Christians and prosecuting them. At the beginning of the 2nd century, Pliny the Younger, while governor of Bithynia-Pontus, faced that dilemma.

He suspected that the secret meetings and common meals held by Christians had a more sinister purpose. Pliny began an investigation and duly executed several Christians who refused to deny their faith. Yet as so often happens in witch-hunts, accusations multiply as each new charge is seized upon as a way of settling old scores. Pliny was next presented with an anonymous pamphlet that named various people who were allegedly Christian. Perhaps now somewhat regretting that he had ever started his inquiries, he asked the emperor's advice. Trajan's reply was both simple and revealing. He instructed Pliny to back off. Christians were not to be sought out; they were to be given every chance to renounce their faith; those who recanted were to be pardoned; no anonymous accusations were to be entertained under any circumstances.

In AD 180, three years after the martyrdoms in Lyon, another group of Christians came before the Roman governor at Carthage. Their leader was one Speratus. Christian eyewitnesses later recorded their version of events in the form of a trial transcript.

Governor: You may merit the clemency of our lord, the emperor, if you return to a right mind.

Speratus: We have never committed any wrong, we have never been party to any wicked deed, we have never uttered a curse, but we have given thanks when ill-treated because we honour our own emperor.

Governor: We also are a religious people and our religion is simple: we swear by our lord, the emperor, and pray for his safety, as you also ought to do.

Speratus: I do not recognise the empire of this world; but rather I serve that God whom with these eyes no man has seen, nor can see.

Governor: Cease to be of this persuasion.

Speratus: But that is evil.

Governor: Do you persist in remaining a Christian?

Speratus: I am a Christian.

Governor: Do you not wish any time for consideration?

Speratus: When right is so obvious there is nothing to consider.

Governor: Have a reprieve of thirty days and think it over.

Speratus: I am a Christian.

As Speratus became increasingly subversive in his remarks, the governor was forced, still unwillingly, to order his execution. This is an important text. It shows that, at least for some Romans, Christians could be regarded as an anti-social group who tried, often rather noisily, to attract attention to themselves. As Speratus' trial reveals, in the face of Roman disinterest, many Christians had to try quite hard to get themselves thrown to the lions.

For the most part, Christians remained on the edges of Roman society and on the margins of its consciousness. In the late 180s, an excited throng mobbed the tribunal of the governor of Asia, Caius Arrius Antoninus. They made it clear that they were all Christians and that they expected the governor without delay to condemn them all to death. Antoninus obligingly had a few of them led away to execution, but as the others ever more insistently demanded the same fate, he turned on this pious crowd in exasperation: 'You wretches,' he cried, 'if you want to die, do you not have cliffs and ropes?'

Importantly too, pagan Romans, in abusing, executing, or just ignoring Christians, demonstrated that they had missed – or simply could not be bothered to recognize – one of the crucial points about this new religion. By lumping Christians together with criminals, robbers, and other undesirables, Romans obscured in their own minds what made this movement exceptional. Christianity was a religion (obviously); but above all else it was a religion of the book. Like Judaism, which the Romans regarded as an odd, ethnic, but undeniably ancient, superstition, Christians relied on a set of sacred texts which they believed to be the word of God. It is this reliance on a set of scriptures that marked out Christianity. It made it more than an anti-social organization likely to crumble in the face of state-sponsored violence.

The establishment of a canonical set of texts was crucial to early Christianity. The New Testament did not appear fully formed. In the two centuries after Christ, different versions were written; different attempts at writing about God hotly debated. A key figure in these disputes was Marcion. Writing in Rome in the early 2nd century, Marcion argued that the Jewish God of the Old Testament was not the same as the Christian God. As he set out to demonstrate in his aptly entitled *Antitheses*, the inconsistencies were simply too great. The God of Moses had created Adam and Eve and thus allowed evil to come into the world. He was responsible for what Marcion regarded as the humiliating process of sexual reproduction, the discomforts of pregnancy, and the pains of childbirth. This Old Testament god, far from being a model of beneficent mercy, had allowed his prophet Elisha to vent his rage on children who had teased him by having them mauled by bears. He had stopped the noonday sun to give Joshua a better opportunity for the slaughter of the Amorites. His ignorance was clearly manifest in his question to Adam in the Garden of Eden: 'Adam, where art thou?' Marcion argued that this was not the sort of question one should expect an omniscient deity to have to ask. Such a god could not be the guarantor of Christian salvation. The revealed creator-god of the Old Testament, with its harsh judicial sanctions and demands for vengeance, was distinct from the God of the New Testament with its promise of liberating grace.

For Marcion, this was a distinction insufficiently recognized by the evangelists. The Gospels needed radical re-editing to make the point. In his new version, Marcion rejected outright the stories of the birth of Christ. In his view, it was inconceivable that God could have been born of a women – virgin or otherwise. Four Gospels too, he contended, produced unnecessary contradictions. Marcion eliminated Matthew, Mark, and John, and expurgated Luke, adding a selection of St Paul's letters. Needless to say, Marcion's ideas did not find general acceptance; in 144 he was expelled from the church in Rome. That is unsurprising: after all, Marcion's project went to the heart of this new religion. If Christianity was to be based on a book, then what should that book look like?

Outside the Christian fold these arguments surrounding the creation of a book that in some way defined a divinity were mostly ignored. When Speratus came before the governor in Carthage, he had a satchel under his arm. The governor asked: 'What have you got in that case?' Speratus replied: 'Books and the letters of Paul, a just man.' But the governor showed no further interest. It was only at the very end of the 3rd century, when the Christian church was a widespread and well-organized institution, that the importance of these documents was realized. In 303, another transcript of proceedings against Christians shows Roman authorities looking for books. In Cirta (modern Constantine in Algeria), Felix, the head of the town council, confronted Catullinus and Marcuclius, junior officials from the local church.

Felix: Bring out the scriptures which you possess so that we can obey the orders and command of the emperors.

(Catullinus produced one reasonably large volume.)

Felix: Why have you given me one volume only? Produce the scriptures which you possess.

Catullinus and Marcuclius: We don't have any more because we are sub-deacons. The readers have the books.

Felix: Show me the readers!

Catullinus and Marcuclius: We don't know where they live.

Felix: If you don't know where they live, tell me their names.

Catullinus and Marcuclius: We are not traitors; here we are, order us to be killed.

Felix: Arrest them.

But this is not a story of martyrdom. Pressure is exerted and the sub-deacons change their mind. Eventually the chief magistrate, having located the readers, retired satisfied with several volumes of religious material.

These proceedings formed part of the persecution by the emperor Diocletian. This was the most effective attempt by the Roman government to deal with Christianity. By seizing books rather than people, Diocletian went to the core of this new religion. It is not surprising that later Christian writers should have referred to these years as 'The Great Persecution'. In the end, the Church survived: Christianity was low on Diocletian's list of priorities; by the end of the 3rd century, the Church was a strong, tightly knit body, and many confronted by the Roman authorities were able successfully to pass off other books as their sacred texts. But the lesson of the Great Persecution was important. It clearly exposed to all, and especially to those imperial officials charged with executing Diocletian's orders, Christianity's dependence on the written word.

This was a lesson not lost on the emperor Constantine. In 312, ten years after Diocletian's Great Persecution, Constantine became the first Roman emperor to embrace Christianity. A key element in Constantine's subsequent public support of his new religion was a concern to establish a firm and testable basis for belief. His aim was to end the debates on the nature and number of the scriptures and to define the Christian God. Constantine was remarkably successful. Faced with a bitter dispute on the divinity of Christ, he summoned the first Mediterranean-wide, ecumenical conference of bishops. They met in June 325 at the lakeside town of Nicaea in north-western Turkey. It is principally thanks to Constantine's coercion of those Christian leaders assembled at the Council of Nicaea that the 'Nicene Creed' was first drafted:

> I believe in one God, Father Almighty, Maker of heaven and earth,
> And of all things visible and invisible: And in one Lord Jesus Christ,
> the only-begotten Son of God, Begotten of his Father before all

worlds, God of God, Light of Light, Very God of very God, Begotten, not made, Being of one substance with the Father, By whom all things were made.

This statement remains the basic formula which modern Christians of all major denominations continue to use in expressing and affirming their faith. The Nicene Creed is not to be found anywhere in the New Testament. It is the product of a much later drive to define Christianity as a system of beliefs, a means of imposing unity on the Church as an institution.

For many who did not share the emperor's beliefs, Constantine's open profession of Christianity must have come as an unpleasant surprise. Looking back – with all the advantages of hindsight – they might perhaps have regretted the previous nonchalant indifference of many Romans. Some no doubt wished that more Christians had been thrown to more lions. But treating Christians like criminals missed the central point of Christianity. It obscured its fundamental reliance on language, on the scriptures, on the Word. It failed to prevent the growth of a sect of fanatics, self-righteously convinced of their own beliefs; a sect that gained both identity and adherents through its glorification of the martyrs, many slaughtered in one of the most symbolically significant spaces in a Roman town. On reflection, it would have been far better to have let the Christians go. Throwing them to the lions certainly provided good entertainment, but it was ultimately counter-productive. If the Roman authorities in the first two centuries AD had been really interested in suppressing Christianity, a much more effective strategy would have been to ignore individual Christians and instead to have seized and burned their books.

Chapter 6
Living and dying

Through the keyhole

The House of Menander was one of the smartest residences in Pompeii. It occupied over half a city block in the southern part of town, roughly mid-way between the forum and the amphitheatre. Its size (at around 1,700 square metres), its lavish decoration, its carefully planned layout, and its expensive furnishings, together reflected both the resources and the tastes of its owner.

The houses excavated at Pompeii and Herculaneum (both near modern Naples in southern Italy) are remarkable for their fine state of preservation; they offer a precious opportunity to understand more closely how the well-off might have lived. Sealed by the volcanic debris that smothered the town following the eruption of Vesuvius in late August AD 79, the House of Menander stands fixed in time; a moment in the Roman past forever frozen.

This house was built to impress. Entering from the street through a grand front door (4.15 metres high, flanked by pilasters), the visitor had an immediate impression of space and grandeur. The vestibule (*atrium*) was large and airy (two storeys high with a floor area of 73 square metres); an opening in the roof (*compluuium*) was

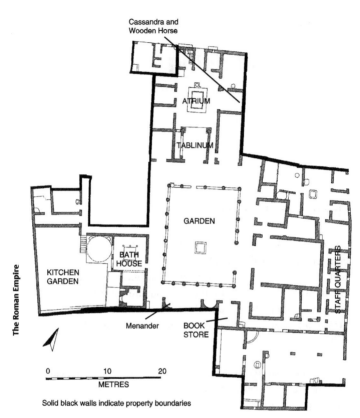

The Roman Empire

16. Ground-plan of the House of Menander, Pompeii

surrounded by terracotta gutter-spouts in the shape of dolphins.
When it rained, water spurted noisily into a white marble pool
(*impluuium*) below, draining into a cistern underneath. From the
front door the visitor could see 40 metres into the house: across the
atrium, past the columns that framed the entrance to an inner hall
(*tablinum*), and beyond to the back of a walled garden surrounded
by a colonnade.

17. View through the *atrium* to the walled garden, House of Menander, Pompeii

This vista was carefully contrived. An optical illusion increased the apparent depth of the house: the nearest pair of columns (at the entrance to the *tablinum*) was taller than the second pair (part of the northern colonnade); those furthest away (the colonnade on the other side of the garden) were both more closely spaced and partly obscured by a low parapet, thus seeming shorter and even more distant than in fact they were. The visitor's gaze was drawn into the house, through zones of alternating light and shade (the *atrium* lit by the *compluuium* above; the covered *tablinum*; the open courtyard; the roofed colonnade), past the lush vegetation and wild animals painted on the low parapets around the garden, and then up to real scenery, topped by nearby mountain peaks.

These elaborate visual conceits were accentuated by an equally carefully devised decorative scheme. Most of the surviving work is associated with various repairs and alterations made in the years following a severe earthquake in AD 62. Reconstruction progressed slowly (perhaps through a shortage of skilled labour); certainly, there is ample evidence that nearly 20 years later, right up until the time of the eruption, there were still builders on site. By then the main rooms had been refurbished in the latest style. In the *atrium* the walls were plastered and painted with large red panels and yellow surrounds; this theme was transposed in the *tablinum* with its yellow panels and red surrounds. In the centre of the red panels in the *atrium* theatrical masks were delicately depicted; on the yellow ground, charming scenes of birds, fruit, and waterfowl; above, a series of painted panels offered a portfolio of views of fantasy landscapes and grand country houses.

To the east of the *atrium*, in a large alcove (3.45 metres wide and 3.75 deep), the spaces between the panels (here, like the *tablinum*, yellow with a red surround) were each filled by a painted niche; in front – continuing the artful illusion – an elaborate picture 'hung' in a dark-purple 'frame'. All three of these scenes show events connected to the sack of Troy, vividly described to Dido and her court by the refugee Aeneas on his arrival in Carthage. On the back

18. Wall-painting of Cassandra and the Trojan Horse, alcove off the *atrium*, House of Menander, Pompeii

wall, directly facing the viewer, a cheering crowd of Trojans hauls the wooden horse towards the city. Heedless of their fate, and ignoring the warnings of the priestess Cassandra (who is dragged roughly away), they make ready to bring the horse into Troy through a breach in the walls.

These paintings are beautiful in themselves; the costly decorative scheme pleasing to the eye; but it also tested the education of any visitor: would the general reference to Virgil's *Aeneid* (specifically Book II) be understood? Could the better educated discern where the artist, perhaps as carefully commissioned, had deviated from Virgil's text? (In the *Aeneid* Cassandra confronts the wooden horse inside Troy, not outside the walls.) The literary preferences of the owner were also expressed in the decoration of the rear (southern) wall of the garden colonnade. Here, in the central of three spacious niches, idealized portraits of three great playwrights were painted. The only one that can securely be identified is a seated figure of Menander, the famous early 4th-century BC author of Greek comedies, after whom the house is now named.

For those who could appreciate such things, the garden, its paintings, and the colonnade made a clear intellectual statement. Here was everything that might be associated with a literary salon in the house of a much wealthier man: a secluded place for private study (appropriately decorated with playwrights), a colonnade for reading and discussion, a larger room for recitations (several of a suitable size opened off the colonnade), and a library (perhaps the room immediately to the left of the three garden niches; inside holes in the plain, white plaster indicated that shelf-brackets had been fixed to three walls). A small, self-contained bath building next to the garden added to a sense of civilized luxury. Here too the owner asserted a connection between himself and an even more privileged world. The House of Menander offered in miniature the same facilities as might be found in any grand country house (like those illustrated on the walls of the *atrium*). The literary allusions, in both architecture and decoration, also marked out the kind of guests – cultured, wealthy, educated, leisured – who might be expected to be entertained in this part of the house; or whom the owner might wish to flatter by introducing to such surroundings as if they were already familiar.

The House of Menander was elegantly designed; by turns, its subtle use of space drew visitors in, courted their approval, and presented a series of social and intellectual challenges. Its decorative scheme demanded educated interpretation (some no doubt admired in judicious silence). These tests could be carefully graded. Light, wooden partitions might exclude visitors from certain parts of the house or increase their pleasure and sense of privilege at being admitted to view yet another impressive room. Fittings in the wall show that the alcove (with its views of Troy) could be screened off, as could the entrance to the *tablinum*. Between the *tablinum* and the colonnade were found square, bronze pivot-settings and hinges from a set of wooden folding doors. The full vista, from the *atrium* to the central niche in the far wall of the garden, was not always on display: the house might be opened up in the warm summer months, and then only for more distinguished visitors.

In addition to the careful placing of physical barriers, the house was policed by a retinue of slaves and servants. A visitor would first encounter the janitor (*ostiarius* or *atriensis*) who slept in a small, plainly decorated room to the left of the front door. Others would regulate progress, or block any further passage, a *nomenclator* (literally, 'name-caller') announcing visitors as they entered the space in which their host had chosen to receive them. No visitor passed through any of the service areas. In the House of Menander these were clearly set apart. Off one side of the garden colonnade, a long corridor and steps gave access to the staff quarters (with its own street entrance); from the other side, another long, angled corridor led to the kitchens. The main kitchen was well equipped: a hearth protected by a masonry hood; in the corner, a large sink whose outflow flushed a latrine in the adjacent room; back along the corridor, nine steps led down to a sunken garden with herbs and vegetables planted out in circular beds. The contrast with the central part of the house was inescapable. The kitchens and staff quarters were carefully hidden away (no inviting vistas here), their decoration rarely more than a coat of coarse plaster. Compared to the lavish brilliance of the reception rooms, they were designed to be invisible.

While the main service areas were marginalized, this does not mean that all domestic activity was entirely excluded from view, as it might have been, for example, in a grand Victorian residence. In the House of Menander the colonnade was also used for open-air cooking (the remains of braziers were found) and for storage. The large jars of wine and olive oil were not hastily tidied away before visitors arrived. Rather, what mattered was the careful regulation of access. From that point of view, the House of Menander eloquently articulated an ascending register of social distinction. Some visitors might never progress beyond the *atrium*, not even catching a glimpse of the garden; others would be warmly welcomed and conducted through the house to join a gathering, perhaps in the colonnade; those particularly favoured would be entertained in ones or twos in one of the smaller, exquisitely appointed rooms. Regrettably, the identity of the owner of this fine residence is not known, but his self-evident wealth places him firmly amongst Pompeii's elite. Like his well-off friends, he owned a house which both complemented and reinforced his social position.

The houses of the elite were not designed as secluded, private places withdrawn from the competitive concerns of the outside world. Rather, in towns throughout the Roman empire, they were built as showy stage-sets on which the owner could further that competition by putting himself on controlled public display to a select audience. No doubt the House of Menander impressed many of its visitors, at least in that narrow social circle which dominated a moderately important town in southern Italy. Yet, for all its clever architectural contrivance and literary pretensions, it would not have been much admired by the really rich, who possessed stately country houses – not merely wall-paintings of them. At best, they might have smiled indulgently at the imitation of the luxuries of truly cultivated living. At worst, they might have regarded the House of Menander as a vulgar attempt to ape a society all too obviously far beyond its owner's experience and finances.

The facts of life

For many modern visitors wandering through the houses of Pompeii or Herculaneum, or walking reflectively along the streets in Ephesus, Aphrodisias, or Lepcis Magna, or any of the other well-preserved sites across the Mediterranean, it is attractive to think that an intimate connection might be forged with at least some of the inhabitants of the Roman empire. Towns like Pompeii seem to reveal so much about the routine of daily life and (perhaps even more striking) something of the sheer ordinariness and apparent familiarity of the ancient world: from designer courtyard gardens to kitchen sinks and vegetable plots; from the time taken by builders to complete a construction job to the anxious concern of a host to impress his guests with the modernity and fashionable good taste of his home. But – as thinking about the House of Menander also makes clear – there are strict limits to such exercises in well-meaning empathy. However similar to our own concerns some of the very human activities of the ancient world might at first sight seem to be, they must be set alongside habits, attitudes, and expectations that make Roman society fundamentally different from the developed, industrial world of the early 21st century.

The Roman empire was dogged by disease and death. Average life expectancy at birth was between 20 and 30 years, roughly one-third of the rate prevailing in modern, Westernized societies. Such a calculation rests less on direct ancient evidence, which is patchy and often poor, than on the assumption that it is reasonable to think of the Roman world following trends common to underdeveloped countries, well known from early 20th-century studies in India and China. At the very least, these help to set parameters. An average life expectancy at birth below 20 years would have resulted in rapid population decline; on the other hand, one above 30 years would make the Roman empire more demographically successful than any known pre-modern society under comparable environmental, social, and economic conditions.

Statistical models can act as helpful guides to understanding populations. They have the advantage of establishing a clear framework for thinking about probable age structures, fertility, and mortality rates. The disadvantage of such generalized abstractions is that they can only reflect probabilities. By definition, models flatten out individual experiences and the inevitable fluctuations across time, from region to region, and between various social groups. These particularities are best exposed by specific investigations: the examination of skeletal evidence from Roman cemeteries (although adults are much more likely to be better preserved than children), or the plotting of ages recorded on epitaphs (although in some cases these records can be shown to be distorted, more closely reflecting cultural preferences for selective commemoration than patterns of actual mortality).

The 'model life table' most commonly applied to the Roman empire is conventionally known as 'Model West, level 3'. It assumes both a stationary population (that is, with a zero growth rate and a constant age structure) and one stable over time (that is, without the effects of either migration or plague). The two columns on the left in Figure 19 track a notional cohort of 100,000 females at five-year intervals from birth to age 85. The third column gives the average remaining life expectancy at those same five-year intervals. The fourth column gives the percentage of the population in each age group.

The patterns are striking. On this model, only half of all babies survive to age 5; the mortality rate is highest in the months immediately after birth, with about one-third of newborns dying before their first birthday. Those who survive to age 5 have, on average, a good prospect of living another 40 years. Such high mortality results in a young population. The average age in Model West, level 3 is 27.3 years for females and 26.2 for males; or, put another way, just over 40% of the population are less than 20, only 4% are 65 years or older. Again, these figures have no pretensions to exactitude; rather, they should be seen as falling within a broader band of probability. That said, within the limitations of a model life table, they offer a valuable sense of the likely proportional relationships between age cohorts. In crude terms, in Roman society the young generally outnumbered the old by somewhere around ten to one; in sharp contrast, this ratio in modern, Westernized societies is under three to one.

Age	100,000 Cohort	Remaining Life Expectancy	% in Age Group
0	100,000	25.0	3.21
1	69,444	34.9	9.53
5	54,456	40.1	10.53
10	51,156	37.5	10.00
15	48,732	34.2	9.46
20	45,734	31.3	8.81
25	42,231	28.7	8.10
30	38,614	26.1	7.36
35	34,886	23.7	6.62
40	31,208	21.1	5.91
45	27,705	18.4	5.22
50	24,389	15.6	4.52
55	20,661	13.0	3.75
60	16,712	10.4	2.91
65	12,175	8.4	2.03
70	7,934	6.4	1.23
75	4,194	4.9	0.58
80	1,644	3.6	0.19
85	436	2.5	0.04

19. **Model Life Table, West level 3, Female**

There is a plausible match between this demographic model for the Roman world and the best surviving evidence. These data, spanning the 1st to the 3rd centuries AD, come from just over 300 returns filed with the local authorities in Roman Egypt as part of a periodic census of the province's population. Preserved on these scraps of papyrus are the details of nearly 1,100 registered persons. The returns suggest an average life expectancy at birth of between 22 and 25 years, with roughly one-third of the population less than 15 years old. These figures, at the lower end of the 20- to 30-year range for average life expectancy in the Roman empire, perhaps also reflect the consequences of a high population density in the fertile and disease-prone Fayum (south of the Nile delta), the region from which two-thirds of the surviving census data come. It is reasonable to assume that the differing ecological conditions around the Mediterranean (arid land, marshes, mountains, plains) would have had an impact on the life expectancy of their particular populations.

Yet, even taking into account environmental variation, it is unlikely that the wealthy necessarily fared significantly better than the rural poor. Under the empire the Senate in Rome had a stable membership of around 600, sustained by a regular annual entry of 20 ex-quaestors (former holders of the most junior magistracy) aged, on average, about 25. This inter-linked pattern of death and recruitment implies that ex-quaestors might normally be expected to survive into their mid-50s and, more broadly, a corresponding average life expectancy at birth in the high 20s. It is likely that the preferential access to superior resources enjoyed by the most privileged members of Roman society was offset by the long periods spent in highly infectious environments such as army camps and crowded urban centres. An analysis of the ages of 30 emperors (from the 1st to the 7th centuries) who died of natural causes indicates an average life expectancy at birth of 26.3 years. For all their riches and power, Roman emperors, even if they successfully avoided assassination, could not hope to live significantly longer than their subjects.

These statistics offer a general impression of the Roman population. Above all, they underscore the persistent incidence of death, particularly amongst infants and the young. Disease was ever-present. The major likely causes of death are familiar from pre-industrial Europe: dysentery and diarrhoea; fevers such as cholera, typhoid, and malaria; pulmonary illnesses such as pneumonia and tuberculosis. The high mortality rate also reflects generally poor nutrition, low standards of hygiene, a cramped urban population in which infection spread rapidly, and (in marked contrast to many early modern nation states) the impossibility, in a large and under-governed empire, of the central authorities being able to impose any strict quarantine. In AD 165, a Roman army returning from campaign in Persia introduced smallpox permanently into the Mediterranean world. The plague lasted for 25 years, and may have wiped out up to 6 million people, roughly 10% of the empire's population.

Harsh mortality rates placed a considerable burden on the reproductive capabilities of Roman women. It is self-evident that in order to maintain a stable population, on average, each woman reaching menarche (the time at which she is physiologically able to conceive) must bear one daughter who also reaches menarche. In a society with high infant mortality, the number of live births needed to satisfy this inexorable demographic demand rises sharply. On average (again using Model West, level 3 as a useful indicator of probabilities), 2.5 female live births are required to maintain a stable population, or for each woman at least five children altogether.

The Egyptian census data reveal a number of ways in which that population group responded to such severe reproductive pressure. On the whole, women married early; on average at just under 20 years. This seems to have been common practice. Funerary inscriptions from the western provinces of the empire (analysed on the reasonable assumption that an unmarried woman is more likely to be commemorated by her parents and a married woman by her husband) indicate an average age at first marriage in the late teens or early 20s. Marriage was also a means of spreading the reproductive burden as widely as possible. In Egypt, 60% of women were married by the age of 20, the remainder by 30. Marriage was near universal. There were very few spinsters in the Roman empire.

The Egyptian data also display a close relationship between fertility and fecundity, that is between the birth rate and the physiological capacity of women to bear children. The birth rate remained roughly stable between the ages of 20 and 35, declining steeply after 45. In marked contrast to normal practice in modern, Westernized societies, there is no evidence of the deliberate cessation of procreation after either the birth or the survival through infancy of a certain number of children. Married women continued to fall pregnant for as long as they were able. Some were remarkably successful. The Egyptian census returns attest couples with as many as eight children. The overwhelming majority declare between zero and three children, but, of course, these returns do not record the number of infant deaths in each family. Moreover, in a stationary population, one-fifth of marriages are childless, and a further one-fifth have only one or more daughters. Behind these cold statistics lies the palpable pain of parents desperately attempting to secure their succession into the next generation. In the mid 2nd century AD, the senator and distinguished orator Marcus Cornelius Fronto lost his first five children in early infancy. In an anguished letter to his former pupil, the emperor Marcus Aurelius, Fronto movingly expressed his sorrow at his failure to start a family.

> I have lost five children in, for me, the most wretched of circumstances. For I lost all five one by one, in each case losing an only child, suffering these bereavements in succession so that I never had a child born to me unless I had been deprived of another. Thus I always lost children without any left behind to console me and, with my grief still fresh, I fathered others.

The risks of high mortality vitiated any reliable, long-term family planning. The majority of those recorded in the Egyptian census data lived in some kind of extended household whose membership might change significantly and suddenly. In one household (from the census of AD 187–188) a married couple have living with them their own daughter, an adult son and daughter from the husband's two previous marriages, and the wife's son and daughter from her previous marriage. Families extended horizontally to embrace those in the same generation or the offspring of previous marriages; it was much less common for them to include a third generation, such as grandparents, for any length of time. These aggregations reflected the consequences of an overall high mortality rate, again unpredictable and highly variable in its impact on individual families. The averages alone make for stark reading: perhaps up to one-third of children lost their fathers before reaching puberty; over half became fatherless before the age of 25; the average 10-year-old had only a one in two chance of having any of his grandparents alive; fewer than 1% of 20-year-olds had a surviving paternal grandfather.

Taken together, these patterns of mortality, marriage, child-bearing, and extended families mark out an experience utterly alien to industrialized societies with much higher life expectancy, much lower birth rates, and the pressing social and financial obligations of supporting an ageing population. The contrasts are significant: surveying the Roman empire, modern eyes might be most immediately struck by the relative absence of old people; the pervasive presence of teenagers; the incidence of orphaned children; and, above all, the distressingly high number of dead babies. This was a society in which it was reasonable to think that (if they survived childhood) most people's lives would have run their course by their mid-40s. Such an expectation also carries with it a radically different sense of the passage of time, of the trajectory of an individual's career (after all, elite high-flyers entered the Senate at 25), and of what might reasonably be achieved or experienced in a generation. In the 170s AD, the emperor Marcus Aurelius, writing in his journal (known to posterity as his *Meditations*), reflected on the dull repetitiveness of human existence. In Marcus' melancholic reckoning, a lifetime of 40 years was sufficient to comprehend the tedium of eternity.

> Look back at the past and at all the changes in the present; it is also possible to foresee the future, for it will be precisely the same and cannot escape from the rhythm of the present. Hence to study a man's life for forty years is the same as studying it for ten thousand years. For what more will you see?

Far from the madding crowd

Most modern imaginings of the Roman empire understandably concentrate on the elite. It is pleasant to picture ourselves walking with princes, offering counsel to the powerful, luxuriating in the grand residences of the rich, appreciating the works of Virgil,

Tacitus, or Plutarch alongside those *cognoscenti* for whom they were first written. In this there is nothing to be ashamed. Indeed, these are experiences which most Romans would have envied. In a Mediterranean-wide population of some 60 million, the wealthy perhaps numbered no more than 200,000.

There are, of course, other enthusiasms. The extensive archaeological remains of the Roman military – its weapons, its armour, and, above all, the forts still standing along Hadrian's Wall in northern Britain and the Rhine frontier in Germany – have inspired some to recreate the daily routine of serving legionaries. These too are minority pursuits. The army under Marcus Aurelius in the late 2nd century AD perhaps totalled 500,000 men, less than 1% of the empire's population. A wider perspective is offered by the magnificent ruins of Roman towns. Certainly, as at Pompeii, it is possible to establish some reliable sense of what life might have been like – at least for around 15% of the empire's population.

The majority of the inhabitants of the Roman empire lived and worked on the land. Land was not only the main source of subsistence in the ancient world, it was also the principal index of wealth. Land was concentrated in the hands of the well-off. A register from the very beginning of the 2nd century AD, surviving from the unremarkable town of Ligures Baebiani in southern Italy, records contributors to a scheme promoted by the emperor Trajan to support a select group of citizen children. The register indicates that 3.5% of the richest landowners held 21.3% of the land (one individual held 11.2%). At the other end of the scale, 14% of the poorest landowners owned only 3.6% of the holdings listed. The size of these estates is difficult to determine. The register from Ligures Baebiani gives only capital values; nor is it known what area it covers. In addition, only properties worth enough to allow their owners to participate in Trajan's scheme were included. The smallest farms, omitted from the register altogether, may have been less than 2.5 hectares. This was the maximum size of plots allotted to Roman citizens who settled conquered territory in northern Italy in the early 2nd century BC. From the 1st century AD veterans (discharged after 25 years' service in the legions) were established in purpose-built towns across the empire and assigned holdings of up to 5 hectares. These colonial ventures left their mark on the provincial landscape: the regular, chessboard pattern of ancient farms is still visible in large tracts of the Tunisian countryside.

Agriculture depended on the peasantry. Only on large estates in Italy, Sicily, southern Gaul, and parts of North Africa did slave labour make any significant contribution. For the most part, the fields were worked by owner-occupiers and their families, by tenant farmers, and by wage labourers. These are overlapping categories. A small proprietor might supplement his income by working on a nearby estate during the harvest. Indeed, the size of the plots allotted to veterans, too small for self-sufficiency, particularly in areas of poor-quality arable land, assume their owners will be able to find other employment. Inevitably, the methods and style of cultivation adopted by peasant farmers, whether as owner-occupiers or tenants, were subject to the physical constraints of climate and terrain: from the cycle of inundation and irrigation in the Nile valley (the most productive area in the empire) to the rain-fed fields of northern Italy or southern France (fertile enough to permit crop rotation rather than require biennial fallow); from the 'run-off' agriculture of the high steppe and pre-desert zones in North Africa (where an elaborate network of canals and terraces distributed water stored after spring rains) to the heavy, wet soils of Britain and the Rhine-Danube provinces.

In the Mediterranean basin, the basic crops were cereals (chiefly barley and wheat), dry legumes (broad beans, peas, chickpeas, lentils), vines, and olives. Dry legumes provided vitamin B2 and calcium, absent from cereals; the olive was a major source of fat, oil, lighting, and soap. A smallholder might also keep pigs (for meat), goats (for cheese), and a few sheep (particularly for manure). Cattle were rare. In the semi-arid Mediterranean lowlands where good arable land was in relatively short supply, large-scale animal husbandry was simply uneconomical. It placed too great a strain on food and water resources. It is perhaps then unsurprising that for many classical writers the raising of livestock was principally associated with far-flung frontier provinces such as Britain and the nomadic peoples living beyond the Rhine-Danube. A diet rich in beef and dairy products was a sure indication of barbarism.

Typically, peasant farming aims to trade maximum production against minimum risk. In much of the Mediterranean, a wide variety of crops was grown in several fields scattered across a broken, hilly landscape. The diversification of plant types and the fragmentation of land acted as a buffer against the chances of crop failure. Careful storage helped ensure adequate supplies throughout the year. Individual farmers down on their luck might also be able to rely on neighbours whom they had perhaps once bailed out in similar circumstances. But for all their thrift, ingenuity, and mutual support, hunger was never far away. In the mid 2nd-century, Galen, one of the most famous ancient doctors whose writings survive, vividly recalled the effects of food shortage on the rural areas around his home town of Pergamum (in western Turkey). Those in the countryside first slaughtered their livestock (which they could no longer feed), then they consumed the acorns which had been stored in pits as winter food for their pigs. Galen noted that, even in famine conditions, few died of starvation, but rather of secondary infections following the consumption of unwholesome substitute foods such as the shoots of trees and bushes, bulbs, and boiled fresh grass.

> Numerous fevers occurred ... defecation was foul smelling and painful, and there followed constipation or dysentery; the urine was acrid or indeed foul-smelling, as some had ulcerous bladders. ... Those to whom none of these things happened all died either from what was evidently inflammation of one of the internal organs or because of the severity and malignity of the fevers.

Despite often harsh environmental conditions and near endemic malnutrition, those on the land were surprisingly resilient in the face of hardship; but theirs was a fragile economy which might suddenly be broken by unpredictable crop failure, drought, or flood, or by the unreasonable demands of landlords, creditors, or tax collectors. Some peasants weathered these crises; some succumbed to death, disease, or debt; others slipped from owning their own farms to become tenants, or from tenants to landless labourers. Their sons perhaps looked to join the army with the expectation that, if they survived 25 years' service in the legions, they would receive their own plot. Many veterans were settled near the garrison town in which they had served, often far away from where they had grown up. And in their new home – like most other people – they continued to work the land.

Smallholders in the Roman empire were a silent majority. They erected few inscriptions; they were commemorated by few epitaphs; their humble, wooden farmsteads have mostly perished without trace; they rarely feature in surviving literary texts, except perhaps as rustic yokels whose puzzlement in the face of cultivated urbanity was sure to raise a laugh. Yet the wealth of the Roman empire depended on those who laboured in the countryside. Their meagre surpluses, extracted as rents or taxes, funded a peacetime army stationed on the frontiers and underwrote the network of cities which gave the empire its administrative and cultural coherence. Roman history (for both educated contemporaries and ourselves) understandably concentrates on emperors, wars, conquest, the rich and powerful, and the remarkably impressive achievements of an urban civilization. These deserve our attention, and may merit our admiration. That said, it can sometimes too easily be forgotten that the stability and prosperity of this vast, Mediterranean superstate rested squarely on the reluctant backs of sweating peasants. History is not just about what has chanced to survive, or what catches the attention of historians. In the face of so much glittering, imperial magnificence, it is always salutary to reflect that most inhabitants of the Roman empire lacked sufficient resources to leave behind any lasting memorial.

Chapter 7
Rome revisited

Pax Britannica

On 11 May 1911, Francis Haverfield (Camden Professor of Ancient History in the University of Oxford) delivered his inaugural address as President of the newly founded Society for the Promotion of Roman Studies. Haverfield found it necessary to justify setting up a learned society: he noted that many might find the whole enterprise 'done to satisfy the grumbles of a few specialists'. He was acutely aware that in the past, while such societies had been responsible through their journals for publishing 'good work', it was also fair to say that 'a vast mass of rubbish has been printed with it'; moreover, Haverfield wondered whether 'individualist England' was the best place to advance a programme of 'collective study and research'.

Against these possible objections, Haverfield mounted a robust defence. He insisted on the complexity of Roman history and the need for teams of experts to assess and evaluate properly the surviving evidence. It was time to limit the influence of the enthusiastic amateur.

> We in England have a poor, perhaps a disastrous, conception of learning ... It is not merely that people think the learned man a social nuisance or an oddity ... But the English have a special

indifference to learning as such. They find no use for it; they believe that any Englishman can go where he likes and achieve what he wishes without training and without knowledge.

But Haverfield had no intention of imprisoning ancient history within an ivory tower closely guarded by specialists who might sneer at any attempt to make their discipline accessible. The real justification for the Society for the Promotion of Roman Studies was its contemporary social and political relevance. For Haverfield, the need to understand Roman history as fully and as accurately as possible, and to communicate that understanding, was never more pressing than at the beginning of the 20th century.

> Roman history seems to me at the present day the most instructive of all histories . . . it offers stimulating contrasts and comparisons . . . Its imperial system, alike in its differences and similarities, lights up our own Empire, for example in India, at every turn.

The degree to which a comparative study of British and Roman imperialism might prove instructive was a matter of debate. At best, Britain and Rome stood in an awkward relationship. Many commentators were quick to point out that the differences between the two empires were so great as to deny any useful parallel: the British empire was larger and dispersed across the globe; its means of communication were more rapid and reliable (from the mid-1860s, the electric telegraph linked Britain and India); its armaments and methods of warfare were technologically far superior; its industrial, commercial, and manufacturing capabilities significantly more sophisticated. Most pressing of all, any comparison also needed to confront the disquieting fact that Britain – for all her subsequent imperial success – had been a province of the Roman empire. The conquerors had themselves once been conquered.

Spearheading a patriotic response to the Roman invasion of Britain was the transformation of Boudica, one of the leaders of the failed revolt by the Iceni in AD 60, into Boadicea, the potent symbol of a nationalist refusal to submit to foreign tyranny. One empire's defeated rebel was to be refashioned as another's heroine. The culmination of this metamorphosis was the imposing statue by Thomas Thornycroft completed in 1871 and erected in bronze on the Embankment in London in 1902. With a dramatic gesture of defiance, Boadicea stands at the reins of a scythed chariot (archaeologically unattested) leading her people against the Roman foe.

This was a project in which Albert, the Prince Consort, expressed a close interest. While Thornycroft was working on the sculpture, Albert visited the studio and lent horses from his own stables to serve as models. Both patron and artist were concerned that this

20. Thomas Thornycroft, bronze sculpture, *Boadicea*, Embankment, London

Boadicea should appear as regal as possible, strongly suggestive of a young Queen Victoria. As a final flourish, William Cowper's stirring poem, *Boadicea, An Ode*, first published in 1782, near the end of the American War of Independence, was quoted on the statue's pedestal.

> Rome shall perish – write that word
> In the blood that she has spilt;
> Perish hopeless and abhorr'd,
> Deep in ruin as in guilt.
>
> Then the progeny that springs
> From the forests of our land,
> Arm'd with thunder, clad with wings,
> Shall a wider world command.
>
> Regions Caesar never knew,
> Thy posterity shall sway,
> Where his eagle never flew,
> None invincible as they.

For a nation at the head of an expanding empire, such stirring stories in praise of native resistance were not without their ambiguities. In 1857, British rule in India was shaken by a series of uprisings conventionally known as 'The Indian Mutiny'. Any comfortable sense of the British empire as a cooperative enterprise was abruptly challenged by the brutal death of unarmed civilians. At Cawnpore (now Kanpur), south of Lucknow, men, women, and children were lined up in front of trenches and mercilessly massacred by Indian rebels. Two years later, in 1859, the poet laureate, Alfred, Lord Tennyson, in a strikingly revisionist image, imagined Boadicea as a bloodthirsty barbarian driving her army on to further atrocities. No heroine here: this was a British mutiny against Roman rule.

Burst the gates, and burn the palaces, break the works of the statuary,
Take the hoary Roman head and shatter it, hold it abominable,

Cut the Roman boy to pieces in his lust and voluptuousness,
Chop the breasts from off the mother, dash the brains of the little one out,
Up my Britons, on my chariot, on my chargers, trample them under us.

As a tale either of legitimate pacification or justified resistance, the myth of Boadicea inevitably involved images of violence, invasion, and savagery. Against these stood a more pacific account of Britain's incorporation into the Roman empire. On this view, it was imperial Rome that had first civilized Britain. In *A School History of England*, published in 1911, Rudyard Kipling and C. R. L. Fletcher made the point in uncompromising terms.

> The Romans introduced into all their provinces a system of law so fair and so strong, that almost all the best laws of modern Europe have been founded on it. Everywhere the weak were protected against the strong. . . . Temples were built to the Roman gods; and country-houses of rich Roman gentlemen . . . these gentlemen at first talked about exile, shivered and cursed the 'beastly British climate', heated their houses with hot air, and longed to get home to Italy. But many stayed . . . and into them too the spirit of the dear motherland entered, and became a passion.

For Kipling and Fletcher, conquest was undoubtedly a good thing. Their only criticism of the Romans was that they had not extended their civilizing rule over all of Scotland or Ireland.

In many ways, *A School History of England* epitomized a theme that had run through much Victorian thinking about Roman Britain. In 1861, William Bell Scott completed a series of eight murals on subjects from local history for Wallington Hall in Northumbria. The first showed the building of Hadrian's Wall at the beginning of the 2nd century AD. Here a commanding Roman centurion, with his military standard beside him, directs local labourers; behind, a legionary repels the attempts of hostile natives to halt this impressive work of imperial construction.

21. William Bell Scott, mural, *The Building of the Roman Wall*, Wallington Hall, Northumbria

The cycle of murals made it clear that such improving endeavours still continued: the final scene – *Iron and Coal: The Nineteenth Century* – offered an equally heroic view of the industrial achievements of modern Tyneside. On the walls above the murals, Scott painted roundels portraying local worthies: here George Stephenson, the pioneer of the steam railway, and the Roman emperor Hadrian found themselves side by side, united in their concern to bring prosperity and civilization to northern England (and a wider empire) through their enthusiastic promotion of engineering.

Certainly, this was an attractive way of thinking about imperial rule.

In a study first published in 1901 – *The Ancient Roman Empire and the British Empire in India* – the Oxford historian, lawyer, and distinguished Liberal politician James Bryce suggested close parallels between the successes of both empires: both had excelled in 'the maintenance of a wonderfully high standard of internal peace and order'; both in their impressive construction of roads and railways had revealed themselves to be 'a great engineering people'; both had achieved successes in war and government which revealed a similar 'dash and energy and readiness to face any odds which bore down all resistance'. These more certain comparisons between the two empires had the advantage of seeming to offer a convincing historical justification for Britain's presence in India, but they also provoked yet more uncomfortable questions. In 1905, in a lecture to the British Academy on *The Romanization of Roman Britain*, Francis Haverfield had argued that one of the reasons for the success of the Roman empire was its rapid and effective 'assimilation of the provincial populations in an orderly and coherent civilization'.

> That was the work of the Empire. ... Above all, the definite and coherent civilization of Italy took hold of uncivilized but intelligent men, while the tolerance of Rome, which coerced no one into conformity, made its culture the more attractive because it was the less inevitable.

These issues were key to the presidential address delivered to the Classical Association in January 1910 by Evelyn Baring, the Earl of Cromer. The Association had been formed in 1903 expressly to promote 'the well-being of classical studies' and 'to impress upon public opinion the claim of such studies to an eminent place in the national scheme of education'. In his lecture on *Ancient and Modern Imperialism*, Cromer, who had recently retired after a distinguished colonial career in India and Egypt, drew explicitly on his own experience in government: 'Being debarred, therefore, from speaking to scholars as a scholar, I thought that I might perhaps be allowed to address the Association as a politician and an administrator.' For Cromer, while there were many points of comparison between the two empires (and here he followed closely the earlier arguments of James Bryce), it was clear that the 'problem of assimilation' was one that marked out an unbridgeable difference between the Romans in Britain and the British in India. 'The comparative success of the Romans is easily explained. Their task was far more easy than that of any modern Imperial nation.'

In Cromer's view, the sheer diversity of India, its many languages, religions, and races, set it apart from anything the Romans had ever encountered. In addition, strongly felt divisions in race and colour between conquerors and conquered were a significant bar to any assimilation:

> The foundations on which the barrier wall of separation is built . . . are of so solid a character, they appeal so strongly to instincts and sentiments which lie deep down in the hearts of men and women, that for generations to come they will probably defy whatever puny, albeit well-intentioned, efforts may be made to undermine them.

Under such circumstances, the only responsible course was to ensure 'the steadfast maintenance of British supremacy'.

> To speak of self-government for India . . . is as if we were to advocate self-government for a united Europe. It is as if we were to assume that there was a complete identity of sentiment and interest between the Norwegian and the Greek, between the dwellers on the banks of the Don and those on the banks of the Tagus. The idea is not only absurd; it is . . . impracticable.

Such views did not go undisputed. A few months later, in May 1910, the Oxford branch of the Classical Association invited Lord Cromer to a special meeting to debate the issues raised by his address. Haverfield, who opened the discussion, suggested that Cromer's emphasis on race and colour had been misplaced. The difficulty was that British rule in India confronted advanced societies 'whose thoughts and affections and traditions and civilization had crystallized into definite form'. In Haverfield's view (perhaps here thinking of his work on Roman Britain), the ability of an imperial power to assimilate its subjects was limited to 'uncivilized or incoherent units'. Even if correct in his conclusions about the imperial future of India, the basis on which Cromer had founded his arguments was at least open to question.

More substantial objections were raised by another Oxford ancient historian and archaeologist, D. G. Hogarth. If history held any lesson, Hogarth suggested, it was in the observation that the Roman empire had 'begun with a period of non-assimilation', had conceived a 'desire to assimilate', and had then progressed to a third stage of 'active assimilation'. The issue was not principally one of race or colour; rather, the British empire should be regarded as being 'still in the first stage of Imperialism'. Only when there was good evidence of 'more or less complete social uniformity' would there be 'a sufficient basis for comparison between the two Empires'. Regrettably, the published minutes of the Association's meeting offer no means of gauging either the audience's or Lord Cromer's reaction to these arguments. Nor to Hogarth's even more provocative conclusion that, in his view, it would evidently be some time before the British developed an advanced system of colonial rule sufficiently mature to be able to match the 'conspicuous success' of the Roman empire.

Romanità

For the Italian fascist leader Benito Mussolini, the Roman empire was free of any disconcerting ambiguity. In a speech delivered in March 1922, and published by Mussolini's own newspaper *Il populo d'Italia* ('The People of Italy') on 21 April, he set out his vision of Romanness – *romanità*.

> Rome is our starting point and our point of reference; it is our symbol or, if you will, our myth. We dream of a Roman Italy: one

which is wise and strong, disciplined and imperial. Much of the immortal spirit of Rome is born again in fascism.

Seven months later, Mussolini was invited by the Italian king, Vittorio Emanuele III, to form a new government. For a revolutionary leader, already preparing for civil war, this was not a particularly dramatic way to seize power. On learning of the news in Milan, Mussolini hurriedly ordered his blackshirt militiamen to march on Rome. Mussolini himself followed, catching the overnight train; well rested, he arrived in Rome in his sleeper car on the morning of 30 October.

The myth of a liberating 'March on Rome' was swiftly created. Photographers were ready to record the arrival of the blackshirts. *Il populo d'Italia* colluded in the manufacture of a heroic struggle, an armed insurrection, and the creation of 3,000 'fascist martyrs' who died in the noble cause of overthrowing a corrupt administration. Ancient history was seen to have repeated itself. Here was a second Julius Caesar who had wished to enter the city on horseback surrounded by his supporters. Mussolini actively encouraged these parallels. In interviews given to the German journalist Emil Ludwig between 23 March and 4 April 1932, he confessed, 'I love Caesar. The greatest of all men who have ever lived.' Writing in *Il populo d'Italia* the following year, he declared:

> This, this too, is an age which can call itself Caesarian, dominated as
> it is by exceptional personalities who again assume for themselves
> the powers of the State for the good of the people . . . just as Caesar
> marched against the senatorial oligarchy of Rome.

The assassination of Caesar on the Ides of March 44 BC Mussolini regarded as 'a disaster for mankind'. In his revision of Roman history (to be taught in Italian schools), Brutus and Cassius were to be cast as agents of an oppressive, reactionary minority seeking to suppress the true champion of popular liberty. The Caesarian cause was only re-established with the victories of Octavian/Augustus, Rome's first emperor. This, above all, was the imperial Rome that

Mussolini aimed to revive. The declaration of war against Ethiopia in October 1935 was presented as a step in the recreation of a Roman empire. This was, in Mussolini's view, nothing less than a 'Fourth Punic War', an assertion of Italian control over the Mediterranean which, in Roman imperial phrase, he insisted on calling *mare nostrum* – 'our sea'. At the beginning of May 1936, the Ethiopian capital, Addis Ababa, was occupied by Italian forces. This was regarded as a sufficient reason to declare a triumph: the public were not informed that most of Ethiopia remained unconquered, or that poison gas had been used, or that Mussolini had authorized 'a systematic policy of terrorism and extermination' to eliminate any further resistance. At 10:30 p.m. on 9 May, from the balcony of the Palazzo Venezia, his headquarters in the centre of Rome, Mussolini addressed a jubilant crowd.

> Italy finally has its own empire . . . An empire of civilisation and of humanity for all the populations of Ethiopia. This is in the tradition of Rome, which after it had conquered them, joined those people to its own destiny. . . . In this certain hope, raise high, O legionnaires, your standards, your swords, and your hearts to salute, after fifteen centuries, the reappearance of empire upon the fated hills of Rome.

For Mussolini, the centrepiece of the resurgence of *romanità* was the city of Rome itself. In his interview with Emil Ludwig, he declared expansively that, 'to my mind, architecture is the greatest of all the arts, for it is the epitome of all the others'. To Ludwig's suggestion that this was indeed a very Roman sentiment, he remarked, 'I, likewise, am Roman above all.' Mussolini was concerned that the ancient grandeur of Rome should be laid bare in a kind of open-air museum to its imperial greatness. In 1931, a commission instructed to prepare a strategic masterplan was ordered not to shy away from proposing the large-scale demolition of buildings and the rehousing of those living in the city's old quarter. The accumulation of 'centuries of decadence' was to be swept away; neither medieval houses nor baroque churches were to impede the revelation of 'a greater Rome'.

The modern appearance of the city is due in great part to Mussolini. The ancient monuments stand out so clearly – to the delight of the tourist – precisely because the surrounding 'sordid picturesque' (in Mussolini's description) was systematically demolished.

> My ideas are clear, my orders are exact ... Rome must strike all nations of the world as a source of wonder: huge, well organised, powerful, as it was at the time of its first empire under Augustus. . . . The thousand year-old monuments of our history must stand out in appropriate solitude like giants.

The Via dell'Impero (Avenue of the Empire) – now less polemically called the Via dei Fori Imperiali (Avenue of the Imperial Forums) – which runs in a straight line from the Palazzo Venezia is entirely a fascist creation. It cut a path through the medieval city to create a clear view of the Colosseum from Mussolini's headquarters. Above all, it provided the necessary monumental space for military parades.

Rome was not only to be recreated on the ground; its wider imperial glory was also celebrated in a great exhibition to commemorate the 2,000th anniversary of the birth of Augustus. The *Mostra Augustea della Romanità* (Augustan Exhibition of Romanness), which opened in Rome on 23 September 1937, contained over 3,000 plaster models of monuments and buildings scattered across the empire. One of the most remarkable was a 1:250 scale model, covering 80 square metres, of the city of Rome at the beginning of the 4th century AD. Never had so much Roman imperial architecture been concentrated in one place; the exhibition aimed to reconstruct for its visitors a coherent vision of an empire restored; its impressive ruins – at least in miniature – made whole again.

Of the one million visitors to the *Mostra Augustea*, amongst the most impressed was Adolf Hilter. Hitler visited Rome from 3 to 9 May 1938. Arriving at night, he was driven through the centre of the city, brilliantly illuminated for the occasion. Over the next two days Hitler visited the *Mostra* twice (the second time at his specific request) and toured extensively the recently exposed ancient monuments of the city. Mussolini's achievements in Rome strengthened Hitler's own resolve completely to rebuild Berlin. Thirteen years earlier, in his autobiographical manifesto *Mein Kampf*, he had complained that the German capital lacked sufficient grandeur, its most important buildings were 'the department stores of a few Jews and the headquarters of a few corporations'. In their place, Hitler demanded public architecture that would 'defy the challenge of time', just as the Colosseum in Rome had 'survived all passing events'. Berlin should be a city even more 'breathtaking' than Rome, 'our only rival in the world'.

The results of this vision for a new Berlin (which Hitler renamed 'Germania') are visible in the models designed by Albert Speer, the Nazis' chief architect. In its scale, monumentality, and evident concern to create vast ceremonial spaces, Speer's plan seems determined to out-build Mussolini. Strikingly too in its individual buildings, whose domes, arches, and porticoes frequently quote Roman architectural forms, this new Berlin aimed to surpass the imperial Rome so painstakingly reconstructed in all its pristine glory in the white plaster models of the *Mostra Augustea*.

This was didactic architecture at its most intimidating and oppressive. For Hitler in Berlin, as for Mussolini in Rome, urban planning was not only a concrete expression of their debt to the Roman empire, it was, above all, a public proclamation of their claim to be the heirs and restorers of *romanità*. As *Mein Kampf* unequivocally advised its readers:

> Particularly in the teaching of history we must not be deterred from the study of Antiquity. Roman history, correctly understood in its broadest outlines, is, and remains, the very best teacher, not only for today, but probably for all times.

22. **Albert Speer, scale model of Germania, the new Berlin, north-south axis looking towards the Volkshalle**

Screening Rome

The Roman general Crassus (Laurence Olivier), unsuccessful in his attempts to seduce his slave Antoninus (Tony Curtis), turns to watch the troops leaving Rome on their way to crush a slave rebellion led by Spartacus (Kirk Douglas).

> There, boy, is Rome – there is the might, majesty, the terror of Rome. There is the power that bestrides the known world like a colossus. No man can withstand Rome, no nation can withstand her . . . There's only one way to deal with Rome, Antoninus: you must serve her, you must abase yourself before her, you must grovel at her feet, you must – love her.

The version of the Roman empire offered by Hollywood to its audiences in the 1950s was clear in its essentials. For the most part, it was unencumbered by the doubts and disputes that had characterized British debates on the merits of empire in India. Rather, it aimed to set its face against the fascist glorification of Rome promoted by (the now defeated) Hitler and Mussolini. In its place, Hollywood offered a vision of an absolutist state, dissolved in its own luxury, brutally committed to the suppression of liberty.

In Hollywood, Rome's rulers were unbalanced madmen. In *Quo Vadis* (first released in 1951), the emperor Nero (Peter Ustinov) is a pastiche of a great dictator. In part, Nero is Hitler. He relentlessly pursues the extermination of the Christians. Nero's holocaust will wipe them from the face of history itself: 'When I have finished with these Christians . . . history will not be sure that they ever existed.' In part, Nero is also Mussolini. In a long tradition of absolute monarchs as megalomaniac urban planners, he is obsessed with creating a new Rome. The magnificent scale model which the emperor unveils to his astonished court was borrowed by the film's producers from the Italian government. The model had originally been made for Mussolini's great *Mostra Augustea della Romanità*.

In part too, Nero is Stalin. As the faceless narration at the opening of *Quo Vadis* sonorously intones:

> With this power inevitably comes corruption . . . No man is sure of

23. Nero (Peter Ustinov) shows his court plans for rebuilding Rome, from *Quo Vadis* (1951)

his life. The individual is at the mercy of the state. Murder replaces justice . . . there is no escape from the whip and the sword.

These images provide the basic cinematic vocabulary of Hollywood's representations of imperial Rome. Ridley Scott, the director of *Gladiator* (2000), confirmed that his staging of the emperor Commodus' victory celebrations was deliberately intended to recall Leni Riefenstahl's *Triumph of the Will* (1935). The parallels between Commodus' parade of power in Rome and Hitler's arrival at a Nazi rally in Nuremberg are unmistakable. Both scenes open with aerial views of monumental buildings and cheering crowds, both offer shots from the viewpoint of the central figure, the camera angles making Commodus and Hitler seem larger than life. In an explicit quotation of the moment in Hitler's progress when he is offered flowers by a little girl, Commodus on the steps of the Senate House is presented with bouquets by children. In Ridley Scott's Rome, the Senate House faces the

Colosseum across a vast square filled with the massed ranks of soldiers. This grandiose vision of the architecture of domination owes most to Hitler's plans for a new Berlin. Rome in the 2nd century AD, with its narrow streets and densely built Forum, was never like this. It only came close in 1932 when Mussolini drove his processional Via dell'Impero straight through the centre of the city.

A strong sense that the enterprise of empire is fatally flawed dominates Hollywood's Rome. Other possibilities may be suggested, but never fulfilled. In *The Fall of the Roman Empire* (1964), the emperor Marcus Aurelius holds out the promise of a multi-cultural world: 'Wherever you live, whatever the colour of your skin, when peace is achieved it will bring to all, *all*, the supreme right of Roman citizenship . . . A family of equal nations.' However rousing the sentiment, the failure to translate this vision into a real political programme is certain.

For Hollywood, Rome is irredeemable. In *Gladiator*, a dying Marcus Aurelius again attempts to avert the inevitable. He declines to confer the succession on his son, Commodus (Joaquin Phoenix), instead instructing the general Maximus (Russell Crowe) to restore the Republic and rescue a 'fragile dream which could only be whispered'. In Rome itself the outspoken Senator Gracchus pointedly observes that, 'the Senate is the people . . . chosen from among the people, to speak for the people'. (Gracchus' claim, directly echoing the traditional language of American republicanism, should be appreciated for what it seeks to convey, rather than being dismissed as an obviously gross historical error.)

But *Gladiator* fails to rise to the political challenge. Maximus is neither shrewd courtier nor committed revolutionary. Above all, he yearns to return to his farm in Spain. Commodus, learning of Marcus Aurelius' plans, kills his father and proclaims himself emperor. Maximus narrowly avoids execution, but can do nothing to save his family, cruelly slaughtered on Commodus' orders. Now a

24. Rome reconstructed, a view from the Senate House, from *Gladiator* (2000)

wounded fugitive, Maximus becomes a gladiator, driven by a desire to avenge his wife and son. The unquestioned rightness of this quest for retributive justice by a politically alienated loner is part of *Gladiator*'s unambiguous celebration of the supremacy of family values. Commodus' unfitness to rule is explained by his dysfunctional relationship with his imperial father who, he complains, never hugged him properly as a child; Commodus' sister, Lucilla, acts to protect her son, even if she must betray others to do so; Maximus' surrogate 'family' of fellow gladiators succeed in the arena precisely because they form a loyal brotherhood; the death of both Commodus and Maximus in a final climactic duel in the Colosseum fulfils the hero's demand for vengeance and allows him, in a final dream-like sequence, to be reunited with his wife and son in the afterlife.

These are well-worn themes. In *The Fall of the Roman Empire*, the hero Livius Metellus (Stephen Boyd), who survives his duel with Commodus, is offered the throne. To shouts of 'Hail, Caesar!', he walks away in disgust. The future lies not in the tainted public space of the imperial court, but with his beloved Lucilla (Sophia Loren) in a private, introspective world of their own. In *Quo Vadis*, the hero Marcus Vicinius (Robert Taylor) is responsible for deposing Nero; he watches the legions of the next emperor, Galba, enter the capital. Newly converted to Christianity, Marcus recognizes the importance of a strict division between church and state. His new religion will not be a catalyst for social reform. Rather, it confirms his retreat from politics: here Christian values are, above all, family values. Marcus, seen at the beginning of the film as a young bachelor back from the wars driving his chariot recklessly through the streets of Rome, now with wife and child leaves the city responsibly at the reins of a sedate, family-sized wagon.

Despite their advocacy of the virtues of the quiet life on the ranch, far away from the tainting perversions of the capital, part of the lasting attraction of 'sword-and-sandal' cinema is that it never entirely escapes what it most seeks to criticize. These films celebrate the epic tales of their own making: for *Ben-Hur* (1959) a full-scale hippodrome was built complete with 40,000 tons of imported sand; in *Quo Vadis* the left-over food from Nero's re-staged banquets was donated to relief agencies for needy children; in *Gladiator* Rome was re-built in digital splendour, only 2,000 spectators in the crowd at the Colosseum were played by extras, the remaining 33,000 were computer-generated. What, above all, distinguishes these films is their lavish, wide-screen grandeur. The huge expense and remarkable technological sophistication of these recreated, celluloid Romes fascinates – rather than repels – the audience.

It is perhaps, then, not surprising that this paradox has also been exploited. The audience for *Quo Vadis* was exhorted to condemn the emperor Nero; but the studio also recognized that in a post-war, newly consumerist America the conspicuous consumption of imperial Rome might also have its attractions. *Quo Vadis* helped promote raincoats, real estate, fire insurance, wallpaper, tablecloths, jewellery, slippers, and pyjamas. Munsingwear, in conjunction with the Knickerbocker Textile Corp., marketed *Quo Vadis* boxer shorts: 'Eight fiery patterns blazing with color . . . The gay designs are plucked right out of the dazzling motion picture of spectacular Roman days.' At last, autocratic excess was made democratically available in main street stores. Wearing his 'full-cut rayon' *Quo Vadis* boxer shorts, every American husband now had the inalienable right to 'make like Nero'.

Modern versions of the Roman empire – in all their excess – should, of course, be enjoyed. At their best, films such as *Quo Vadis*, *The Fall of the Roman Empire*, or *Gladiator* convey something of the sheer spectacle of a triumphal procession, the grandeur of the great houses of the very wealthy, the bloody thrill of gladiatorial games, the terror of battle, the frightening whimsy of autocracy, and the metropolitan magnificence of Rome. More rarely do they capture the Roman sense of their own imperial mission (as discussed in

25. Poster advertising Munsingwear rayon boxer shorts

Chapter 1), or offer a sense of the difficulties and ambiguities
surrounding the exercise and representation of imperial power (as
in Chapter 2), or care to understand the delicate position of
provincial elites (as in Chapter 3). Conquest and resistance are
routinely conceived exclusively in terms of armed force (there is
little room for the more subtle alternatives explored in Chapter 4).
Christianity is presented as fully formed and often openly

Protestant in its outlook and beliefs (the doubts and disputes canvassed in Chapter 5 are quietly swept aside). For the most part too, the cinematic world of the Roman empire is remarkably fit and healthy. Cohorts of well-oiled, muscle-bound extras disguise a society (explored in Chapter 6) beset by poor nutrition, high infant mortality, infectious disease, and low life expectancy.

At the core of Hollywood's cinematic Rome lie intensely personal struggles: celebrations of the supremacy of the individual in the face of a dehumanizing totalitarian régime, tales of the triumph of love (usually pagan stud gets Christian virgin), and the quest for righteous revenge (usually wronged and defiantly heterosexual hero defeats madly decadent and evidently deviant ruler). These attractive combinations are no doubt largely responsible for the continuing popularity of the Roman empire. That should be applauded: but knowingly. It is always worth remembering that it is very unlikely that cheering on rebels, supporting obscure cults, subverting imperial power, or exalting personal freedom as the touchstone of a civilized society would ever have had much box-office appeal for a Roman audience.

For the most part, contemporary recreations of Antiquity – debates on British imperialism in India or the monumental urban fantasies of the 1930s – are best understood as revealing commentaries on the complexities and concerns of those societies which promote them. Under such circumstances, the 'accuracy' of these portrayals of ancient Rome (whatever their claims to authenticity) is of secondary importance. The commercial success of *Gladiator* is a timely reminder that our own visions of the ancient world are still very modern affairs; they lavishly parade our own priorities and problems; they project our own aspirations and anxieties. Like their Victorian and fascist predecessors, 21st-century Romes reveal more about the present than the past. They dress up our dreams and fears in togas. Yet in the end, they can offer only a much less revealing – and in some ways, a much less entertaining – very short introduction to the Roman empire.

The Roman world in the late 2nd century AD

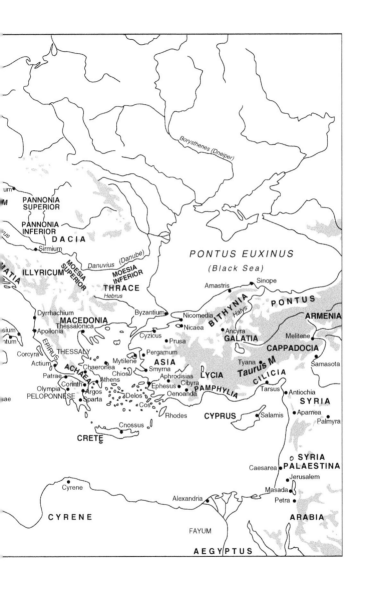

Chronology, 31 BC – AD 192

55/56	Seneca writes *On Mercy*
59	Death of Agrippina
60	Revolt lead by Boudica in Britain
64	Great fire in Rome
64–68	Building of Golden House in Rome
65	Suicide of Seneca
68–69	**Galba**
69	**Otho and Vitellius**
66–70	Jewish revolt
70	Sack of Jerusalem
70s	Dio Chrysostom faces down bread riot at Prusa
71	Titus and Vespasian hold triumph at end of Jewish revolt
74	Suicide of *sicarii* at Masada
69–79	**Vespasian**
77–84	Cnaeus Julius Agrippa governor of Britain
79–81	**Titus**
79	Vesuvius destroys Pompeii and Herculaneum
80	Completion of Colosseum in Rome
81/82	Completion of Arch of Titus in Rome
83	Defeat of Calgacus in northern Britain
81–96	**Domitian**
96–120	Plutarch writes *Parallel Lives*
96–98	**Nerva**
98–117	**Trajan**
100	Pliny the Younger delivers his *Panegyric*
101	Land register from Ligures Baebiani
101–102	First Dacian War
104	Caius Vibius Salutarius funds procession in Ephesus
105–106	Second Dacian War
c. 110	Martyrdom of Ignatius of Antioch in Rome
110–112	Pliny the Younger governor of Bithynia-Pontus
113	Completion of Trajan's Column in Rome

Further reading

Chapter 1: Conquest

Roman Republic

Michael Crawford, *The Roman Republic*, 2nd edn. (London, 1992)

Mary Beard and Michael Crawford, *Rome in the Late Republic: Problems and Interpretations*, 2nd edn. (London, 1999)

Keith Hopkins, *Death and Renewal* (Cambridge, 1983), ch. 2

Peter Brunt, *The Fall of the Roman Republic and Related Essays* (Oxford, 1988)

Augustus

Ronald Syme, *The Roman Revolution* (Oxford, 1939)

Paul Zanker, *The Power of Images in the Age of Augustus* (Michigan, 1988)

Kurt Raaflaub and Mark Toher (eds.), *Between Republic and Empire: Interpretations of Augustus and his Principate* (Berkeley, 1990)

Conquest

William Harris, *War and Imperialism in Republican Rome 327–70 BC* (Oxford, 1979)

Ramsey MacMullen, *Enemies of the Roman Order: Treason, Unrest, and Alienation in the Empire* (Harvard, 1966)

Richard Hingley and Christina Unwin, *Boudica: Iron Age Warrior Queen* (London, 2005)

Aeneid

Philip Hardie, *Virgil's Aeneid: Cosmos and Imperium* (Oxford, 1986)

Stephen Harrison (ed.), *Oxford Readings in Virgil's Aeneid* (Oxford, 1990)

For a good modern verse translation, Robert Fitzgerald (London, 1984)

Chapter 2: Imperial power

Imperial cult

Keith Hopkins, *Conquerors and Slaves* (Cambridge, 1978), ch. 5

Mary Beard, John North, and Simon Price, *Religions of Rome, Vol. I: A History* (Cambridge, 1998), chs 5–7

Simon Price, *Rituals and Power: The Roman Imperial Cult in Asia Minor* (Cambridge, 1984)

Ittai Gradel, *Emperor Worship and Roman Religion* (Oxford, 2002)

Seneca

Miriam Griffin, *Seneca: A Philosopher in Politics* (Oxford, 1976)

Pliny

Andrew Wallace-Hadrill, '*Civilis Princeps*: Between Citizen and King', *Journal of Roman Studies*, 72 (1982): 32–48

Shadi Bartsch, *Actors in the Audience: Theatricality and Doublespeak from Nero to Hadrian* (Harvard, 1994), ch. 5

Suetonius

Andrew Wallace-Hadrill, *Suetonius: The Scholar and his Caesars* (London, 1983)

Nero

Jaś Elsner and Jamie Masters (eds.), *Reflections of Nero* (London, 1994)

Edward Champlin, *Nero* (Harvard, 2003)

Tacitus

John Henderson, *Fighting for Rome: Poets and Caesars, History and Civil War* (Cambridge, 1998), ch. 4

Ronald Mellor, *Tacitus* (London, 1993)

Chapter 3: Collusion

Empire and Provinces

Clifford Ando, *Imperial Ideology and Provincial Loyalty in the Roman Empire* (Berkeley, 2000)

J. E. Lendon, *Empire of Honour: The Art of Government in the Roman World* (Oxford, 1997)

Andrew Lintott, *Imperium Romanum: Politics and Administration* (London, 1993)

Stephen Mitchell, *Anatolia: Land, Men, and Gods in Asia Minor*, 2 vols (Oxford, 1993)

Greg Woolf, *Becoming Roman: The Origins of Provincial Civilization in Gaul* (Cambridge, 1998)

Martin Millett, *The Romanization of Britain: An Essay in Archaeological Interpretation* (Cambridge, 1990)

Greg Woolf, 'Monumental Writing and the Expansion of Roman Society in the Early Empire', *Journal of Roman Studies*, 86 (1996): 22–39

J. B. Ward-Perkins, *Roman Imperial Architecture*, 2nd edn. (Harmondsworth, 1981)

Pliny

A. N. Sherwin-White, *The Letters of Pliny: A Historical and Social Commentary* (Oxford, 1966)

Dio Chrysostom

Christopher Jones, *The Roman World of Dio Chrysostom* (Harvard, 1978)

Chapter 4: History wars

Hadrian

Anthony Birley, *Hadrian: The Restless Emperor* (London, 1997)

Mary Boatwright, *Hadrian and the Cities of the Roman Empire* (Princeton, 2000)

Greeks under the Roman empire

Glen Bowersock, *Greek Sophists in the Roman Empire* (Oxford, 1969)

Susan Alcock, *Graecia Capta: The Landscapes of Roman Greece* (Cambridge, 1993)

Tim Whitmarsh, *Greek Literature and the Roman Empire: The Politics of Imitation* (Oxford, 2001)

Simon Goldhill (ed.), *Being Greek under Rome: Cultural Identity, the Second Sophistic and the Development of Empire* (Cambridge, 2001)

Simon Swain, *Hellenism and Empire: Language, Classicism, and Power in the Greek World, AD 50–250* (Oxford, 1996)

Pausanias

Christian Habicht, *Pausanias' Guide to Ancient Greece* (Berkeley, 1985)

William Hutton, *Describing Greece: Landscape and Literature in the Periegesis of Pausanias* (Cambridge, 2005)

Plutarch

Tim Duff, *Plutarch's Lives: Exploring Virtue and Vice* (Oxford, 1999)

Christopher Jones, *Plutarch and Rome* (Oxford, 1971)

It is worth noting that the *Penguin Classics* translations of Plutarch's *Lives* break up the biographical pairs and omit the formal comparisons; the translation of Pausanias can likewise be misleading, as it has been reordered to suit the modern tourist.

Chapter 5: Christians to the lions

Gladiators

Keith Hopkins, *Death and Renewal* (Cambridge, 1983), ch. 1

Jeremy Toner, *Leisure and Ancient Rome* (Cambridge, 1995)

Thomas Wiedemann, *Emperors and Gladiators* (London, 1992)

Paul Plass, *The Game of Death in Ancient Rome: Arena Sport and Political Suicide* (Wisconsin, 1995)

Keith Hopkins and Mary Beard, *The Colosseum* (London, 2005)

Martyrdom

Glen Bowersock, *Martyrdom and Rome* (Cambridge, 1995)

Daniel Boyarin, *Dying for God: Martyrdom and the Making of Christianity and Judaism* (Stanford, 1999)

Early Christianity

Henry Chadwick, *The Church in Ancient Society: From Galilee to Gregory the Great* (Oxford, 2001)

Robin Lane Fox, *Pagans and Christians* (Harmondsworth, 1986)

Philip Rousseau, *The Early Christian Centuries* (London, 2002)

William Frend, *The Rise of Christianity* (London, 1984)

Chapter 6: Living and dying

Pompeii

Andrew Wallace-Hadrill, *Houses and Society in Pompeii and Herculaneum* (Princeton, 1994)

Wim Jongman, *The Economy and Society of Pompeii* (Amsterdam, 1988)

Paul Zanker, *Pompeii: Public and Private Life* (Harvard, 1998)

P. Veyne (ed.), *A History of Private Life, I: From Pagan Rome to Byzantium* (Harvard, 1987), ch. 1

Demography

Richard Saller, *Patriarchy, Property and Death in the Roman Family* (Cambridge, 1994)

Tim Parkin, *Old Age in the Roman World: A Cultural and Social History* (Johns Hopkins, 2003)

Roger Bagnall and Bruce Frier, *The Demography of Roman Egypt* (Cambridge, 1994)

Walter Scheidel, 'Roman Age Structure: Evidence and Models', *Journal of Roman Studies*, 91 (2001): 1–26

Agriculture

Brent Shaw, *Environment and Society in Roman North Africa* (Aldershot, 1995)

Peter Garnsey, *Famine and Food Supply in the Graeco-Roman World: Responses to Risk and Crisis* (Cambridge, 1988)

Peter Garnsey, *Cities, Peasants and Food in Classical Antiquity* (Cambridge, 1998)

Chapter 7: Rome revisited

Victorian Rome

Catharine Edwards (ed.), *Roman Presences: Receptions of Rome in European Culture, 1789–1945* (Cambridge, 1999)

Richard Hingley, *Roman Officers and English Gentlemen: The Imperial Origins of Roman Archaeology* (London, 2000)

Norman Vance, *The Victorians and Ancient Rome* (Oxford, 1997)

Sam Smiles, *The Image of Antiquity: Ancient Britain and the Romantic Imagination* (Yale, 1994)

Fascism

Alex Scobie, *Hitler's State Architecture: The Impact of Classical Antiquity* (Penn State, 1990)

Peter Bondanella, *The Eternal City: Roman Images in the Modern World* (North Carolina, 1987)

Hollywood

Sandra Joshel, Margaret Malamud, and Donald McGuire (eds.), *Imperial Projections: Ancient Rome in Modern Popular Culture* (Baltimore, 2001)

Maria Wyke, *Projecting the Past: Ancient Rome, Cinema and History* (London, 1997)

Martin Winkler (ed.), *Gladiator: Film and History* (Oxford, 2004)

Jon Solomon, *The Ancient World in the Cinema*, 2nd edn. (Yale, 2001)

Index

Index

ROMAN BRITAIN
A Very Short Introduction
Peter Salway

Britain was within the orbit of Graeco-Roman civilization
for at least half a millenium, and for over 350 years part of
the political union created by the Roman Empire that
encompassed most of Europe and all the countries of the
Mediterranean.

First published as part of the best-selling *Oxford
Illustrated History of Britain*, Peter Salway's Very Short
Introduction to Roman Britain weaves together the results
of archaeological investigation and historical scholarship in
a rounded and highly readable concise account. He charts
the history of Britain from the first invasion under Julius
Casear ro the final collapse of the Romano-British way of
life in the 5th century AD.

www.oup.co.uk/isbn/0-19-285404-6

ARCHAEOLOGY
A Very Short Introduction
Paul Bahn

This entertaining Very Short Introduction reflects the enduring popularity of archaeology – a subject which appeals as a pastime, career, and academic discipline, encompasses the whole globe, and surveys 2.5 million years. From deserts to jungles, from deep caves to mountain tops, from pebble tools to satellite photographs, from excavation to abstract theory, archaeology interacts with nearly every other discipline in its attempts to reconstruct the past.

'very lively indeed and remarkably perceptive … a quite brilliant and level-headed look at the curious world of archaeology'

Barry Cunliffe, University of Oxford

'It is often said that well-written books are rare in archaeology, but this is a model of good writing for a general audience. The book is full of jokes, but its serious message – that archaeology can be a rich and fascinating subject – it gets across with more panache than any other book I know.'

Simon Denison, editor of *British Archaeology*

www.oup.co.uk/vsi/archaeology

ONLINE CATALOGUE
A Very Short Introduction

Our online catalogue is designed to make it easy to find your ideal Very Short Introduction. View the entire collection by subject area, watch author videos, read sample chapters, and download reading guides.

SOCIAL MEDIA
Very Short Introduction

Join our community

www.oup.com/vsi

- Join us online at the official Very Short Introductions **Facebook** page.
- Access the thoughts and musings of our authors with our online **blog**.
- Sign up for our monthly **e-newsletter** to receive information on all new titles publishing that month.
- Browse the full range of Very Short Introductions online.
- Read **extracts** from the Introductions for free.
- Visit our library of **Reading Guides**. These guides, written by our expert authors will help you to question again, why you think what you think.
- If you are a teacher or lecturer you can order inspection copies quickly and simply via our website.